YOUR recipe could appear in our next cookbook!

Share your tried & true family favorites with us instantly at

www.gooseberrypatch.com

If you'd rather jot 'em down by hand, just mail this form to...
Gooseberry Patch • Cookbooks – Call for Recipes
PO Box 812 • Columbus, OH 43216-0812

If your recipe is selected for a book, you'll receive a FREE copy!

Please share only your original recipes or those that you have made your own over the years.

Recipe Name:

Number of Servings:

Any fond memories about this recipe? Special touches you like to add
or handy shortcuts?

Ingredients (include specific measurements):

Instructions (continue on back if needed):

Special Code: **cookbookspage**

Over ↗

Extra space for recipe if needed:

Tell us about yourself...

Your complete contact information is needed so that we can send you your FREE cookbook, if your recipe is published. Phone numbers and email addresses are kept private and will only be used if we have questions about your recipe.

Name:
Address:
City: State: Zip:
Email:
Daytime Phone:

Thank you! Vickie & JoAnn

Tastes Like Home

235 comfort food recipes with a hearty helping of memories, plus, handy kitchen tips

Gooseberry Patch

**An imprint of Globe Pequot
246 Goose Lane
Guilford, CT 06437**

www.gooseberrypatch.com

1•800•854•6673

Copyright 2016, Gooseberry Patch 978-1-62093-188-2

Do you have a tried & true recipe...

tip, craft or memory that you'd like to see featured in
a **Gooseberry Patch** cookbook? Visit our website at
www.gooseberrypatch.com and follow the
easy steps to submit your favorite family recipe.
Or send them to us at:

Gooseberry Patch
PO Box 812
Columbus, OH 43216-0812

Don't forget to include the number of servings your recipe makes,
plus your name, address, phone number and email address. If we
select your recipe, your name will appear right along with it...
and you'll receive a **FREE** copy of the book!

Contents

Dedication

To everyone with fond memories of eating cozy home-cooked meals around the family dinner table.

Appreciation

A big thanks to everyone who generously shared their favorite tried & true recipes for this book.

Rise & Shine

Grandma's French Toast

Kathie Craig
Burlington, WI

Whenever my grandkids will be staying overnight, I buy a loaf of Italian bread for this recipe. The grandkids love to use a whisk to stir it up...they enjoy dipping the bread slices too. It's a fun, hands-on recipe for them. I mix one batch at a time. It's less messy and all the grandkids get a turn to help. I like to use my own grandma's cast-iron skillet...so many memories made!

2 eggs, beaten	1 t. cinnamon
1/3 c. milk	1 T. butter
1 T. sugar	4 slices day-old Italian bread
1/2 t. vanilla extract	Garnish: maple syrup

In a shallow dish, whisk together eggs, milk, sugar, vanilla and cinnamon until blended. Melt butter in a skillet over medium heat. Dip bread into egg mixture on both sides, one slice at a time, coating well. Add bread to skillet. Cook on both sides for about 4 minutes, until golden and egg mixture is set. May keep warm in a 250-degree oven until all slices are cooked. Serve with syrup. Makes 2 servings, 2 slices each.

A yummy topping for French toast...combine an 18-ounce jar of apricot jam with 1/2 cup orange juice in a saucepan. Bring to a boil and stir to blend; serve warm.

Rise & Shine

Oven Apple Pancake

Barb Rudyk
Alberta, Canada

This is a wonderful recipe to make on a cold winter morning. Add a platter of breakfast sausages for a great start to the day!

1/4 c. margarine, sliced
1/4 c. brown sugar, packed
cinnamon to taste
2 apples, peeled, cored and cut
    into 1/4-inch wedges

3 eggs, room temperature
3/4 c. milk
1/2 t. salt
3/4 c. all-purpose flour
Garnish: maple syrup

Place margarine in a 9" pie plate; melt in a 350-degree oven. Remove from oven; stir brown sugar into melted margarine. Sprinkle with cinnamon. Arrange apples in pie plate, overlapping in a single layer. Bake at 350 degrees for 10 minutes. Meanwhile, beat eggs in a bowl; add milk, salt and flour. Mix until blended. Pour batter over apples; return to oven. Continue baking for 20 to 25 minutes, until golden and apples are tender. Cut into wedges. Serve with syrup. Makes 6 servings.

Which apple is best? The tastiest apples for baking are Rome, Jonathan, Fuji and Granny Smith. For salads, try McIntosh, Red Delicious, Empire and Gala.

Lemon Ricotta Pancakes

Paula Marchesi
Lenhartsville, PA

My grandmother used to serve these delicious pancakes every Sunday after church. They were so good that when I grew up and had my own family, I continued the same tradition. My boys loved them as much as I did, and now I serve them to my grandchildren.

1-1/2 c. all-purpose flour
3 T. sugar
1-1/2 t. baking powder
1/2 t. baking soda
1/4 t. salt
1 egg, beaten
1 c. part-skim ricotta cheese

3/4 c. 2% milk
1/2 t. lemon zest
1/2 c. lemon juice
1/2 c. butter, melted
1/2 t. vanilla extract
Garnish: warmed maple syrup,
   powdered sugar

In a large bowl, whisk together flour, sugar, baking powder, baking soda and salt; set aside. In a separate bowl, whisk together egg, ricotta cheese, milk, lemon zest and juice, melted butter and vanilla. Add egg mixture to flour mixture; stir just until moistened. Lightly grease a griddle; heat over medium heat. Pour batter by 1/4 cupfuls onto griddle. Cook until golden on bottom and bubbles on top of pancakes begin to pop. Turn; cook until golden on other side. Serve with warmed syrup and powdered sugar. Makes 4 servings, 3 pancakes each.

To increase the amount of juice you'll get from
a lemon, microwave the whole lemon on high power for
20 to 30 seconds before cutting and squeezing.

8

Rise & Shine

Mom's Healthy Pancakes

Katie Wollgast
Florissant, MO

My grandpa clipped this recipe from a newspaper long ago. These were his favorite pancakes. He gave the recipe to my mom and they became her favorite too. I have grown to love them, not only as delicious pancakes, but also because of the memories that come with them! I serve these with homemade maple syrup or fruit sauce and topped with a spoonful of yogurt.

1 c. all-purpose flour
1/2 c. toasted wheat germ
1 T. sugar
2-1/2 t. baking powder
1/2 t. salt

1-1/4 c. milk
2 T. water
1/2 c. low-fat cottage cheese
Garnish: maple syrup, fruit or
    fruit topping, yogurt

In a large bowl, combine flour, wheat germ, sugar, baking powder and salt; set aside. In a separate bowl, combine milk, water and cottage cheese. Add milk mixture to flour mixture; stir just until moistened. Cook on a lightly greased heated griddle, using about 1/4 cup batter per pancake. When bubbles appear on top, turn. Cook until golden and centers are firm. Serve immediately, garnished as desired. Makes 4 servings, 2 pancakes each.

Garden-fresh berries and peaches are luscious on waffles and pancakes. Frozen fruit is good too and available year 'round. Simmer fruit with a little sugar until it's syrupy. What a scrumptious way to start the day!

Pecan-Topped Coffee Cake

Cassie Hooker
La Porte, TX

My mother used to make this recipe when I was growing up. It is a really good moist coffee cake that's even more delicious the next day.

1 c. margarine, softened
2 c. sugar
3 eggs, beaten
1 c. sour cream

1 t. vanilla extract
2 c. all-purpose flour
1 t. baking powder
1/4 t. salt

In a large bowl, blend together margarine and sugar. Add eggs, sour cream and vanilla; mix well. Add flour, baking powder and salt; mix again. Pour half of batter into a greased Bundt® pan; sprinkle with a little more than half of Topping. Add remaining batter to the pan; add remaining Topping. Bake at 350 degrees for one hour, or until cake tests done with a toothpick inserted near center. Let cake cool in pan for several minutes; turn out onto a cake plate. Makes 10 to 12 servings.

Topping:

1 c. finely chopped pecans
1/4 c. brown sugar, packed

1 t. cinnamon, or more to taste

Mix all ingredients in a small bowl.

A Bundt® coffee cake with a flower-filled vase tucked in the center makes a delightful centerpiece for a casual brunch gathering.

Rise & Shine

Stuffed French Toast Logs
Sylvia Stachura
Mesa, AZ

These delicious cinnamon treats can be prepared ahead of time and refrigerated. In the morning, simply bake and watch the smiles!

24 slices white sandwich bread, crusts removed
2 8-oz. pkgs. cream cheese, softened
2 egg yolks

1-3/4 c. sugar, divided
1-1/2 c. butter, melted
4 t. cinnamon
Garnish: maple syrup, whipped cream

Flatten bread slices with a rolling pin; set aside. In a bowl, beat together cream cheese, egg yolks and 1/2 cup sugar. Spread mixture evenly on bread slices; roll up, jelly-roll style. Place melted butter in a shallow bowl. Combine cinnamon and remaining sugar in a separate shallow bowl. Lightly dip rolls in butter, then in cinnamon-sugar. Place on ungreased baking sheets. Bake at 350 degrees for 20 minutes, until golden. Serve topped with maple syrup and whipped cream. Makes about 6 servings.

No-Sharing Monkey Bread
Jill Ball
Highland, UT

My family loves monkey bread, but whenever I served it, the breakfast table became a scramble for the first piece. So I decided to make individual portions, thus ensuring harmony at breakfast.

12 frozen dinner rolls, thawed
6 T. butter, melted
2 T. corn syrup

1/2 c. brown sugar, packed
2 T. cinnamon

Cut each roll into 6 pieces; set aside. Combine butter and syrup in a bowl; mix well. In a separate bowl, combine brown sugar and cinnamon. Dip dough pieces into butter mixture, then into brown sugar mixture. Place dough in a greased muffin tin sprayed with non-stick vegetable spray, 4 to 5 pieces per cup. Cover tin with sprayed plastic wrap. Let rise until double in size, 15 to 20 minutes. Uncover; bake at 350 degrees for 15 to 20 minutes. Serves 12.

Dad's Crazy Eggs

Catherine Snyder
Blue Springs, MO

We looked forward to Dad making this special breakfast on Saturday mornings. He was a great experimental cook who enjoyed recreating recipes for dishes he'd tasted while traveling. This recipe he perfected over the years. But no one wanted to be on the clean-up crew...Dad had a habit of using lots of dishes while cooking!

1 lb. bacon, chopped
1/2 onion, finely chopped
1 green pepper, chopped
1 c. sliced mushrooms
8 eggs, beaten

1/2 c. milk
2 c. shredded Cheddar cheese
1 tomato, chopped
Garnish: 2 T. fresh parsley
Optional: salsa

In a large deep skillet over medium heat, cook bacon just until crisp. Remove bacon to paper towels and drain, reserving drippings in skillet. Add onion and green pepper to drippings. Cook until tender; drain. Reduce heat to medium-low; add crumbled bacon and mushrooms to skillet. Cook until mushrooms are softened. Whisk eggs with milk in a bowl. Add to skillet and cook until almost set. Remove skillet from heat; sprinkle with cheese and tomato. Place skillet under broiler for 3 to 5 minutes, until cheese is melted and bubbly. Garnish with parsley. Serve with salsa, if desired. Makes 6 servings.

To clean a cast-iron skillet, simply scrub with coarse salt,
wipe with a soft sponge, rinse and pat dry. Salt cleans
cast iron thoroughly without damaging the seasoning
like dish detergent would.

Scrambled Eggs with Ham, Cheddar & Chives

Annette Ingram
Grand Rapids, MI

This recipe has been a family favorite for quite some time. We always make it using leftover Easter ham and the first spring chives in our garden, but it's delicious year 'round. The kids like to roll it up in a tortilla for a take-along breakfast burrito. Enjoy!

2 T. butter, sliced and divided
1-1/4 c. cooked ham, diced
10 eggs
2 T. milk

salt and pepper to taste
1 to 2 T. fresh chives, chopped
1 to 1-1/2 c. shredded sharp
   Cheddar cheese

Melt one tablespoon butter in a large skillet over medium heat. Add ham; cook until golden. In a large bowl, whisk together eggs, milk, salt and pepper. Melt remaining butter in skillet; pour egg mixture into skillet. Cook, stirring occasionally, until eggs are lightly scrambled, about 5 minutes. Shortly before eggs are set, sprinkle with chives and cheese. Cover and let stand until cheese is melted. Makes 4 to 6 servings.

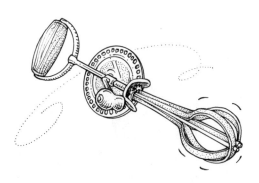

For the best scrambled eggs, don't skimp on the whisking.
Whisk until the yolks are completely blended with
the whites, about 30 to 40 seconds. You'll be rewarded
with soft, fluffy scrambled eggs.

13

Sausage & Grits Casserole

Suzette Rummell
Cuyahoga Falls, OH

*My mother was from Georgia but raised her family in Florida.
She loved her native Georgia catfish and grits and made this
casserole often. We loved the grits...but the catfish, not so much!*

6 c. water
2 c. long-cooking grits,
  uncooked
1/2 c. butter, sliced and divided
3-1/2 c. shredded Cheddar
  cheese, divided

1 lb. ground pork breakfast
  sausage
1 doz. eggs
1/2 c. milk
salt and pepper to taste

Bring water to a boil in a large saucepan over medium-high heat; stir
in grits. Reduce heat to medium. Cover and simmer about 5 minutes,
or until water has been absorbed. Add 1/4 cup butter and 2 cups
cheese; stir until melted. Meanwhile, brown sausage in a large skillet
over medium-high heat; drain and stir into grits mixture. Whisk
together eggs and milk in a bowl; pour into same skillet. Cook and stir
over medium-low heat until eggs are lightly scrambled; fold eggs into
grits mixture. Lightly grease a 3-quart casserole dish; pour grits
mixture into dish. Season with salt and pepper. Dot with remaining
butter; top with remaining cheese. Bake, uncovered, at 350 degrees
for 30 minutes, or until lightly golden and cheese is melted. Makes
6 to 10 servings.

Visit a nearby farmers' market for fresh fruits & vegetables,
baked goods, jams & jellies...perfect for a farm-fresh breakfast!

Rise & Shine

Turkey Sausage Patties

Kathy Courington
Canton, GA

I started making these tasty patties years ago for a lighter version of sausage and my husband loves them. Feel free to season them just the way you like!

1 lb. ground turkey
1 t. salt
1/4 to 1/2 t. nutmeg

1/4 to 1/2 t. ground sage
1/4 to 1/2 t. dried thyme
1/16 t. cayenne pepper

Combine all ingredients in a bowl, adding seasonings to taste. Mix together thoroughly with your hands; form into 12 small patties. Cook patties in a large skillet over medium heat until golden and cooked through. May also place patties on a rack in a shallow pan; bake at 350 degrees for 10 to 15 minutes. Serves 6, 2 patties each.

Broiled Grapefruit Dessert

Joan White
Malvern, PA

My mother-in-law's favorite dessert...perfect for brunch too!

2 grapefruits, halved
1/2 c. light brown sugar, packed

2 T. butter, melted
1 t. cinnamon

With a small, sharp knife, loosen the segments in each grapefruit half by carefully cutting between the fruit and the peel. Cut along either side of each segment to free it from the membrane. Leave segments in their shells. Place grapefruit halves cut-side up in a baking pan. In a small bowl, stir together remaining ingredients. Sprinkle mixture evenly over grapefruit halves. Place under broiler, about 4 inches from heat source. Watching carefully, broil until brown sugar is evenly bubbly, 2 to 3 minutes. Serve immediately. Makes 4 servings.

Come along inside...we'll see if tea and buns
can make the world a better place.
-Kenneth Grahame

Grandma's Eggs Cheddar

Carolyn Deckard
Bedford, IN

*Whenever we were lucky enough to stay overnight at Grandma's
on Christmas Eve, on Christmas morning she would fix
this wonderful breakfast for us. It's still special to me.*

2 green onions, chopped
1 T. butter
10-3/4 oz. can tomato soup
16-oz. pkg. shredded sharp
    Cheddar cheese
1/2 t. dry mustard
1/4 t. dried basil

salt and pepper to taste
3 eggs, beaten
1-1/2 c. milk
4 slices French bread,
    cut 2 inches thick and lightly
    toasted
Garnish: chopped fresh parsley

In a skillet over medium heat, sauté onions in butter until golden.
Reduce heat to low; add soup, cheese and seasonings. Cook and stir
until well blended and cheese is melted. In a bowl, whisk together
eggs and milk; add to cheese mixture. Cook until eggs are lightly set.
Arrange toast in the bottom of a lightly greased 9"x9" baking pan.
Spoon cheese mixture over bread. Bake, uncovered, at 350 degrees
for 15 minutes, or until golden on top. Garnish with parsley.
Makes 4 servings.

Love cheesy recipes, but want to cut down on the calories
and fat? Choose reduced-fat (not fat-free) cheese,
which melts well in hot dishes.

Rise & Shine

Simple Spinach Quiche

Diane Cohen
Breinigsville, PA

*I love to make this quiche for a meatless meal any time
of day, served with a crisp salad and fresh fruit.*

9-inch pie crust
2 eggs, beaten
1 c. milk
1/2 t. salt
1/4 t. pepper

1-1/2 c. shredded Cheddar
   cheese
1/2 c. grated Parmesan cheese
10-oz. pkg. frozen spinach,
   thawed and well drained

Arrange pie crust in a 9-inch pie plate; flute edges and set aside. In a
bowl, whisk together eggs, milk, salt and pepper. Fold in cheeses
and spinach; pour mixture into pie crust. Bake at 350 degrees for
45 minutes, or a until knife inserted into center comes out clean. Cut
into wedges; serve warm. Makes 8 servings.

Bake crustless mini quiches in muffin tins...great for
brunches, and kids will love 'em! When making minis,
reduce the baking time by about 10 minutes and
check for doneness with a toothpick.

17

Granny's Potatoes & Eggs

Julia Chaperon
Bay Port, MI

My granny Julia Salis came from Belgium. Her family was very poor during the war and this is one of the main meals they had. They were lucky to have this for dinner! Now we make it all the time as a quick and tasty breakfast, lunch or dinner, since everyone loves it. This keeps Granny alive in our hearts.

1 T. olive oil
2 T. butter, sliced and divided
4 lbs. potatoes, peeled and cubed

1 clove garlic, minced
8 eggs

Add olive oil and one tablespoon butter to a large skillet over medium-low heat. Arrange potatoes in skillet. Cover; cook for 10 to 15 minutes, adding garlic after 5 minutes, until potatoes are soft and golden. Uncover; add remaining butter and eggs to skillet. Stir well until eggs are scrambled. Cook over low heat until eggs are set, about 2 more minutes. Makes 6 to 8 servings.

For tempting breakfast potatoes that are crisp and golden outside and soft inside, try parboiling. Bring a saucepan of water to a boil; add potato cubes and boil for about 6 minutes. Drain well and pan-fry as desired.

Crisp Potato Cakes

Gloria Kaufmann
Orrville, OH

A very basic potato cake recipe that is easy to make. They're excellent with eggs for breakfast...I often serve these with baked fish for dinner. For a quick start, use refrigerated shredded potatoes.

1 egg, well beaten	3/4 t. salt
1/2 t. onion, grated	2 to 3 potatoes, shredded
3/4 t. baking powder	2 to 3 T. oil

In a bowl, combine egg, onion, baking powder and salt; mix well. Add shredded potatoes and immediately stir well so potatoes do not darken; set aside. Heat oil in a skillet over medium heat. Drop potato mixture by large spoonfuls into skillet. Sauté until crisp, golden and cooked through, about 10 minutes. Serve immediately. Makes 4 servings.

Are family members eating breakfast on the run? Any egg dish turns into a portable breakfast when rolled up in a tortilla or spooned into a pita round.

Sour Cream Muffins with Strawberries

Angie Salayon
New Orleans, LA

I received this recipe from a neighbor who inherited a vintage handwritten recipe book from her mother. The muffins are delicious with strawberries, which are my contribution to the recipe.

1/2 c. butter, softened
4 eggs, well beaten
1-1/2 c. sour cream
2-3/4 c. all-purpose flour
1-1/2 c. sugar
1 t. baking soda

1/2 t. salt
1/8 t. nutmeg
2 c. strawberries, hulled
  and diced
Optional: sugar to taste

In a bowl, blend butter, eggs and sour cream. Gradually add remaining ingredients except berries; mix thoroughly. Fill 24 buttered muffin cups 2/3 full. Bake at 450 degrees for 15 minutes, or until a toothpick tests clean; cool. Place berries in a bowl; add sugar to taste, if needed. Spoon over muffins just before serving. Makes 2 dozen.

Barbara's Best Blueberry Buns

Pamela Elkin
Asheville, NC

My dear friend Barbara shared this delicious recipe with me several years ago. They are so easy to make and are so good.

13-oz. tube refrigerated
  cinnamon rolls
1 c. frozen blueberries, thawed
  and well drained

1/2 c. blueberry preserves
1 t. lemon zest
1/3 c. chopped pecans
small amount milk

Split cinnamon rolls in half horizontally; set aside icing. Spray 16 muffin cups with non-stick vegetable spray. Press each roll piece into the bottom of a muffin cup, about 1/2-inch thick. In a bowl, mix blueberries, preserves and lemon zest. Evenly spoon into cups; top with pecans. Bake at 350 degrees for 10 to 12 minutes, until golden. Cool for 5 minutes; turn out of muffin cups. Thin icing with a few drops of milk; drizzle over buns. Serve warm. Makes 16.

Fruit-Filled Coffee Cake

Diana Krol
Nickerson, KS

This has been a family favorite for more than 30 years.
My son Adam was a 4-H grand champion winner in 1990 using
this recipe! It's delicious and takes very little time to prepare.

1 c. butter, softened
1-1/2 c. sugar
4 eggs
3 c. all-purpose flour

1-1/2 t. baking powder
1-1/2 t. salt
21-oz. can apricot pie filling or
    other favorite flavor

In a large bowl, blend together butter and sugar; beat in eggs, one at a time. In a separate bowl, stir together flour, baking powder and salt. Gradually add flour mixture to butter mixture; blend well to form a stiff batter. Reserving one cup batter, spread batter over an oiled 16"x11" jelly-roll pan. Spoon pie filling over batter; dab reserved batter over pie filling. Bake at 350 degrees for 15 to 20 minutes, until lightly golden. Drizzle Glaze over warm cake; cut into squares. Makes 10 to 12 servings.

Glaze:

1 c. powdered sugar
3 T. milk

1/2 t. almond extract

Combine ingredients in a small bowl; mix until smooth.

Repurpose empty tea tins as planters! To create drainage holes, carefully hammer a thin, sharp nail through the bottom a few times, and place the lid underneath to act as a saucer.

Family Favorite Monkey Muffins

Andria Meyers
Chester, MT

I wanted a snack muffin recipe that was a little healthier for my kids when they were toddlers, so I tweaked a recipe and came up with this. My family loved them even with my healthy additions. They still request them often, several years later! Don't be afraid of the long list of ingredients...they are very easy and are just as good without the wheat germ and flax.

1/2 c. butter, softened
1/2 c. honey
2 eggs, beaten
1 very ripe banana, mashed
2/3 c. creamy natural peanut
    butter
1 T. plain yogurt
1 t. vanilla extract
1 c. all-purpose flour
1 c. whole-wheat flour

1 c. long-cooking oats,
    uncooked
1 t. baking soda
1/4 t. salt
Optional: 2 T. wheat germ,
    2 T. ground flax
1/4 c. shredded coconut
3/4 c. semi-sweet chocolate
    chips

Blend butter and honey in a large bowl. Beat in eggs and banana. Stir in peanut butter, yogurt and vanilla; set aside. In a separate bowl, combine flours, oats, baking soda and salt; add wheat germ and ground flax, if using. Add flour mixture to butter mixture; stir just until moistened. Do not overmix. Fold in coconut and chocolate chips. Fill greased or paper-lined muffin cups 2/3 full. Bake at 350 degrees for 16 to 18 minutes. Makes 1-1/2 dozen.

Looking for an alternative to peanut butter? Try sun butter, made from sunflower seeds, or soy nut butter, made from soybeans. If your child has a peanut allergy, check with his or her doctor first, to be on the safe side.

Delicious Bran Muffins

Virginia Craven
Denton, TX

I like the variety of wholesome ingredients in these muffins, but I really love how delicious and moist they are. They're perfect for a quick breakfast or a snack. The batter can be refrigerated up to two weeks to bake later, which is really convenient.

1 c. boiling water	1 c. sugar
3 c. whole bran cereal	2-1/2 t. baking soda
3/4 c. golden raisins	3/4 t. salt
3/4 c. chopped dates	2 c. low-fat buttermilk
Optional: 3/4 c. walnuts,	1/2 c. canola oil
coarsely broken	1/2 c. applesauce
2 c. all-purpose flour, divided	1 egg, or 1/2 c. egg substitute

In a heatproof bowl, pour boiling water over cereal; stir and let stand. In a separate bowl, combine raisins, dates and walnuts, if using; sprinkle with 1/2 cup flour and toss to combine. In a large bowl, combine remaining flour and other ingredients. Add cereal mixture to flour mixture; mix until moistened. Fold in fruit mixture. Spray a muffin tin with non-stick vegetable spray; spoon batter into muffin cups, filling 2/3 full. Bake at 400 degrees for 18 to 20 minutes. Batter will keep for 2 weeks if refrigerated in an airtight container; stir again and bake as needed. Makes 2 dozen.

For the tenderest muffins and quick breads, stir batter just until moistened...a few lumps won't matter.

Heart-Healthy Baked Oatmeal

Anita Dualeh
Saint Paul, MN

This crumbly cake-like oatmeal is a welcome choice for those who do not care for the texture of traditional cooked oatmeal. Made with olive oil and reduced sugar, it's an updated version of an old recipe. My whole family enjoys it...in fact, my sons think the leftovers make a great dessert!

2 c. quick-cooking oats,
   uncooked
1/4 c. brown sugar, packed
1 t. baking powder
1/2 t. salt
1 egg, beaten

6 T. olive oil
1/2 c. 2 % milk or soy milk
Garnish: sliced bananas or
   other fresh or dried fruit,
   plain yogurt,

In a large bowl, mix together oats, brown sugar, baking powder and salt. Add remaining ingredients except garnish; stir well. Spoon mixture into a greased 9" glass pie plate. Bake, uncovered, at 350 degrees for about 20 minutes, until center no longer looks wet on top. To serve, spoon into cereal bowls; serve warm, topped with fruit and a dollop of yogurt. Makes 4 servings.

Try steel-cut oats in any recipe that calls for regular long-cooking oats. Steel-cut oats are less processed for a pleasing chewy texture you're sure to enjoy.

Apple Cobbler Oatmeal

Katie Majeske
Denver, PA

A few years ago, my son Matt was in an accident and was laid up in bed for several weeks. I would make this oatmeal, pull up a chair beside his bed, and together we would enjoy a warm bowl of comfort. Some days I used steel-cut oats...so good either way!

1 c. old-fashioned or steel-cut
   oats, uncooked
2 c. water
1 apple, cored and diced

1/2 c. milk, or to taste
2 T. brown sugar, packed
2 T. sliced or slivered almonds
cinnamon to taste

In a saucepan, cook oatmeal with water according to package directions. Stir in apple. Remove from heat; divide into 2 cereal bowls. Stir in milk, brown sugar, almonds and cinnamon. Makes 2 servings.

Try stuffed French toast for a new twist. Dip half the bread slices in egg mixture and top with a dollop of fruit preserves. Dip the remaining slices in egg mixture and lay over preserves, pressing down slightly to make a sandwich. Cook on a hot griddle until both sides are golden.

Applesauce Muffins

Amy Bradsher
Roxboro, NC

My kids love muffins, and this recipe is our favorite!
It's sweet, apple-y and delicious hot or cold.

1/2 c. butter, softened
1 c. sugar
2 eggs
2 c. white whole-wheat flour
1 t. baking powder

1/2 t. baking soda
1/4 t. salt
1 t. cinnamon
1 c. applesauce

In a large bowl, blend butter and sugar. Add eggs, one at a time, beating well after each. In a separate bowl, combine remaining ingredients except applesauce; mix well. Add flour mixture to butter mixture alternately with applesauce. Mix until just combined. Spoon into greased muffin cups, filling 2/3 full. Bake at 350 degrees for 20 to 25 minutes. Makes one to 1-1/2 dozen.

A neighborly gesture never goes out of style. Wrap homemade muffins or scones in a tea towel, tuck them into a basket with a jar of jam and deliver to a friend. A sweet gift that says "I'm thinking of you!"

Soups & Breads

to Warm the
Heart

Summer Minestrone Soup

Ramona Wysong
Barlow, KY

I adapted this recipe from one I saw using ingredients I liked.
It's a light soup packed with fresh veggies.

3 T. butter, sliced
1 onion, chopped
1 T. garlic, minced
4 carrots, peeled and diced
2 yellow squash, diced
2 zucchini, diced
dried oregano, basil and parsley
    to taste
seasoning salt, salt and pepper
    to taste

4 c. chicken broth
1-1/3 c. small pasta shells,
    uncooked
2 15-oz. cans diced tomatoes
1 to 2 bunches broccoli, cut into
    bite-size flowerets

Melt butter in a very large saucepan over medium heat. Sauté onion
and garlic until tender. Add carrots and cook for about 10 minutes,
stirring occasionally. Add squash, zucchini and seasonings to taste.
Stir in broth; heat until simmering. Stir in uncooked pasta shells,
tomatoes with juice and broccoli. Simmer until pasta and broccoli are
tender, about 10 to 13 minutes. Makes 6 to 8 servings.

Mix up your own herb seasoning. Fill a shaker-top jar with
2 teaspoons of garlic powder and a teaspoon each of onion
powder, dry mustard, paprika, pepper, dried thyme
and celery seed. Terrific in soups!

Tuscan Soup

Jeanne Caia
Ontario, NY

Always a big hit...you may want to double the recipe!
Serve with warm bread sticks.

2 T. olive oil
1/2 c. onion, peeled and diced
1 carrot, diced
1 redskin potato, diced
2 14-oz. cans chicken broth
1 c. water
1/4 t. dried marjoram

1/8 t. pepper
15-oz. can cannellini beans
2/3 c. tubetti or ditalini pasta,
   uncooked
1/2 head escarole, thinly sliced
Garnish: shredded Parmesan
   cheese

Heat oil in a large saucepan over medium-high heat. Add onion, carrot and potato; cook until lightly golden, about 5 minutes, stirring often. Add broth, water and seasonings; bring to a boil over high heat. Reduce heat to low. Cover and simmer for 10 minutes, or until vegetables are tender. Stir in undrained beans and uncooked pasta; bring to a boil over high heat. Reduce heat to low; cover and simmer for 15 minutes, or until pasta is tender, stirring occasionally. Stir in escarole; heat through. Top with Parmesan cheese. Makes 4 servings.

Don't throw away the rind from a wedge of fresh Parmesan cheese...add it to a pot of simmering soup! The rind will dissolve into the soup, adding rich flavor.

Creamy Tomato Soup

Linda Morceau
Pocasset, MA

My favorite soup as a child was tomato. When I became gluten-intolerant as a young adult, I had to figure out how to make tomato soup for myself and this delicious recipe was the result.

1 onion, diced
2 cloves garlic, minced
1-1/2 t. olive oil
28-oz. can crushed tomatoes
   with basil
10-1/2 oz. can chicken broth

1-1/3 c. water
1/4 t. pepper
3/4 c. whipping cream
1 T. honey
salt to taste

In a large saucepan over medium heat, sauté onion and garlic in oil until tender. Add tomatoes with juice, broth, water and pepper; bring to a fast boil. Reduce heat to low; simmer for 12 minutes. Remove from heat; let cool for 2 minutes. Stir in cream, honey and salt. Additional broth may be added if too thick. Return to low heat; cook for an additional 2 to 3 minutes, until heated through. With an immersion blender or regular blender, blend until completely smooth; serve. Makes 4 to 6 servings.

Try using evaporated skim milk in soups instead of cream... you'll save about 500 calories for each cup replaced. Evaporated milk doesn't need refrigeration, so it's easy to keep on hand.

Basil-Tomato Grilled Cheese   *JoAnn*

*What's better than a grilled cheese sandwich? One that's
chock-full of fresh ingredients from the farmers' market!*

8 slices Texas toast or other
   thick-sliced bread, divided
8 slices mozzarella cheese
2 to 3 roma tomatoes, sliced
2 t. balsamic vinegar

2 T. fresh basil, snipped
salt and pepper to taste
1/4 c. olive oil
3 T. shredded Parmesan cheese
1/4 t. garlic powder

Top 4 slices of bread with 2 slices of cheese each. Arrange tomato
slices evenly over top. Drizzle with vinegar; sprinkle with basil, salt
and pepper. Top with remaining bread slices; set aside. In a cup,
combine oil, cheese and garlic powder; brush over both sides of each
sandwich. Heat a large skillet or griddle over medium heat; add
sandwiches. Cook until golden on both sides and cheese is melted.
Makes 4 sandwiches.

Nothing perks up the flavor of tomato soup like fresh basil!
Keep a pot of basil in the kitchen windowsill and just pinch off
a few leaves whenever they're needed.

Dinner Chowder

LaShelle Brown
Mulvane, KS

This is my all-time childhood favorite recipe! When Mom said we were having this chowder for dinner, we would always get so excited. I still love it, and now that I have a family of my own, they are just as excited when I tell them we are having it for dinner.

2-1/2 c. water
2 c. potatoes, peeled and
   chopped
3/4 c. onion, minced
1/2 c. celery, coarsely diced
2 t. salt, divided
3 T. butter
1/4 c. all-purpose flour

1/4 t. pepper
1/2 t. dry mustard
1-1/2 t. steak sauce
2 c. milk
1 c. canned diced tomatoes
1 T. fresh parsley, snipped
8-oz. pkg. pasteurized process
   cheese, chopped

Bring water to a boil in a medium saucepan over medium-high heat; add potatoes, onion, celery and 1/2 teaspoon salt. Simmer until tender, 10 to 15 minutes; drain. Meanwhile, melt butter in a large saucepan over medium-low heat; sprinkle in flour and stir until smooth. Add remaining salt, pepper, dry mustard, steak sauce and milk to butter mixture; cook and stir until thickened. Stir in cooked vegetables, tomatoes and parsley. Add cheese; cook and stir over low heat until cheese is melted. Makes 4 to 6 servings.

Keep shopping simple...have a shopping list that includes all ingredients you normally use, plus a few blank lines for special items. You'll breeze right down the aisles!

Pinwheel Sandwiches

LaShelle Brown
Mulvane, KS

Pinwheel Sandwiches and soup were my favorite dinner combo when I was young and still are as an adult. They are simple to make. The salty ham paired with the melty cheese makes them so delicious!

8-oz. tube refrigerated
    crescent rolls
4 slices American cheese, each
    cut into 4 squares

8 square slices deli ham

Roll out crescent rolls; pinch seams together to create one large rectangle. Cut dough into 8 equal squares. On each dough square, place one small square of cheese in the center, followed by a slice of ham, then topped with another small square of cheese. Make a one-inch slice in each of the 4 corners of dough square, angled toward the center of the sandwich. Pull the piece of dough from the right side of each slice and fold it to the center of the sandwich, to look like a pinwheel. Fasten with a wooden toothpick, if desired. Place sandwiches on an ungreased baking sheet. Bake at 350 degrees for 10 to 15 minutes, until dough is golden and cheese is melted. Makes 8 sandwiches.

Fast and fun! Whip up several different kinds of sandwiches and cut each one into four sections. Arrange them all on a large platter with chips and pickles...everyone will love the variety and it couldn't be easier.

Hungarian Cabbage & Sausage Soup

Nancy Allen
Bountiful, UT

This soup is total comfort food, and like most soups, it tastes better after a night in the fridge. I've been making this recipe for more than 15 years and everyone loves it. It is always requested for potlucks.

10-oz. pkg. ground pork
    country-style sausage
10-oz. pkg. ground pork Italian
    sausage
2 T. oil
2 onions, sliced
1 green pepper, chopped
2 cloves garlic, minced
1 head cabbage, shredded

2 T. paprika
1 T. dried marjoram
2 t. salt
1 t. pepper
4 c. chicken broth
4 c. water
4 potatoes, peeled and cubed
8-oz. container sour cream
3 T. all-purpose flour

In a large stockpot over medium heat, brown both packages of sausage in oil. Add onions, green pepper and garlic. Cook until tender, about 6 minutes; drain. Add cabbage and cook until soft, stirring occasionally. Stir in seasonings; cook for 3 minutes. Add broth, water and potatoes. Cook until potatoes are tender, about 10 to 15 minutes. Place sour cream in a bowl; stir flour. Gradually stir in a little of the hot soup broth, until sour cream mixture is warmed through. Whisk the sour cream mixture into soup. Reduce heat to low. Simmer without boiling for another 20 minutes. Makes 8 to 10 servings.

Need to add a little flavor boost to a pot of soup? Just add a splash of an acidic ingredient. Start with a teaspoon of lemon or lime juice, or 1/2 teaspoon of cider vinegar, adding a little more to taste as needed.

Sausage & Swiss Chard Soup

Phyllis Pierce
Greenfield, MA

My very favorite soup! This recipe was given to me by my former boss, the Monsignor. It makes a great meal served with crusty bread. You can adjust the heat by using sweet sausage and reducing the amount of red pepper flakes. This soup freezes well.

6 c. water
2 bunches Swiss chard, sliced
    into 1-inch strips and stems
    discarded
4 T. olive oil, divided
6 cloves garlic, minced
1/2 t. red pepper flakes
1 T. tomato paste
4 to 6 links hot Italian pork
    sausage, casings removed
    and sliced 1-inch thick

2 carrots, peeled and diced
1 onion, chopped
2 stalks celery, chopped
28-oz. can diced tomatoes
2 15-oz. cans cannellini beans,
    drained and rinsed
2 14-oz. cans beef broth
2 14-oz. cans chicken broth
salt and pepper to taste

In a large stockpot over high heat, bring water to a boil. Add Swiss chard; cover and return to a boil. Reduce heat to medium-low and simmer for 15 minutes, or until tender. Drain chard in a colander; set aside. Meanwhile, in a large skillet, heat one tablespoon oil over medium-low heat. Add garlic and red pepper flakes. Cook, stirring constantly, for 2 minutes, or just until garlic is golden. Immediately stir in tomato paste; cook for one minute more. Add sausage and 2 tablespoons oil; cook until browned. Drain; remove sausage to a plate and set aside. Add remaining oil, carrots, onion and celery to pot. Cook over low heat until softened. Return sausage and chard to pot. Add tomatoes with juice and beans; stir well. Add broth, salt and pepper. Simmer for 30 minutes, stirring occasionally. Serves 8.

Soups taste even better the next day...why not make
a favorite soup ahead of time? Let it cool thoroughly,
then cover and refrigerate until tomorrow night.
A lifesaver when you've got a busy day coming up!

Village Stone Soup

Janis Parr
Ontario, Canada

*I love the folktale story of Stone Soup. It has wonderful meaning
and is a lesson for all. This soup inspired by the tale will
warm you through & through.*

4 14-1/2 oz. cans chicken broth
5 potatoes, peeled and cubed
1 small butternut squash, peeled
   and coarsely chopped
4 carrots, peeled and coarsely
   chopped
1 onion, coarsely chopped
1 c. celery, coarsely chopped

1/2 c. quick-cooking barley,
   uncooked
salt and pepper to taste
3 cubes chicken bouillon
3-1/2 c. cooked chicken, cubed
14-1/2 oz. can diced tomatoes
1 c. fresh or frozen green peas

In a large soup pot over high heat, combine broth, potatoes, squash,
carrots, onion and celery. Bring to a boil. Reduce heat to medium-low.
Cover and simmer for 20 to 25 minutes, until vegetables are tender,
stirring occasionally. Add barley, seasonings, bouillon cubes, chicken,
tomatoes with juice and peas. Return heat to high; bring to a boil.
Reduce heat to medium-low; cover and simmer for 12 to 15 minutes,
until barley is tender. Serve piping hot. Makes 12 servings.

Let the tale of Stone Soup inspire a fun get-together!
Invite everyone to bring a favorite veggie, while you
provide a bubbling stockpot of broth. While the soup simmers,
play games together for an old-fashioned good time.

Soups & Breads
to Warm the Heart

One-Egg Muffins

Helen McKay
Edmond, OK

When I was growing up in Utah, my mother would make these muffins on cold winter nights to serve with her homemade soup. They are simple to make and oh-so good hot from the oven with butter and homemade jam.

1/4 c. shortening
1/4 c. sugar
1 c. milk
1 egg, beaten

2 c. all-purpose flour
4 t. baking powder
1/2 t. salt

Combine all ingredients in a bowl; stir until moistened well. Spoon batter into greased muffin cups, filling 2/3 full. Bake at 375 degrees for about 30 minutes, until golden. Makes 8 to 12.

Butter Crust Beer Bread

Lynn Foley
Branson, MO

A quick & easy bread that's good with just about anything. We love it with homemade vegetable soup.

2 c. self-rising flour
3 T. sugar
12-oz. can regular (not light) beer or non-alcoholic beer

1/4 c. butter, melted

In a bowl, mix flour, sugar and beer until well blended and a sticky, dough forms, about one minute. Spoon dough into a greased 8"x5" loaf pan. Bake at 350 degrees for 30 minutes. Remove from oven; pour melted butter over the top. Return to oven and bake 30 more minutes until lightly golden. Cool bread in pan before removing. Makes one loaf.

Keep freshly baked bread warm and toasty. Tuck a piece of aluminum foil into a bread basket before adding the bread.

Chicken Corn Soup

Shirley Condy
Plainview, NY

This is the most delicious chicken soup and very easy to make.
It has an unusual kind of dumpling called dough balls. I received
the recipe from an Amish lady in Pennsylvania.

1 lb. chicken breast
4 c. water
4 cubes chicken bouillon
10-3/4 oz. can cream of celery
   or chicken soup
1-1/2 t. salt, divided
1/2 c. celery, diced

1/2 c. onion, diced
2 16-oz. cans creamed corn
16-oz. can corn, drained
1 c. all-purpose flour
1/4 t. baking powder
1 egg, beaten

In a large pot over medium-high heat, combine chicken, water and
bouillon cubes. Bring to a boil. Reduce heat to medium-low and
simmer for 45 minutes to one hour, until chicken is tender. Pull
chicken off bones, reserving broth; dice chicken and return to broth.
Add soup, one teaspoon salt, celery, onion and corn; simmer for
15 minutes. For dough balls, combine flour, baking powder, egg and
remaining salt in a bowl; mix thoroughly. Sift dough through your
fingers into the soup. Stir and simmer for 15 minutes. Serves 6 to 8.

The most indispensable ingredient of all good home cooking...
love, for those you are cooking for.
- Sophia Loren

Gram's Macaroni Soup

Victoria Mitchel
Gettysburg, PA

This recipe has been in my family for years. I loved it as a child and now my own children do as well...there is nothing like it with a slice of warm bread! Gram used the tomatoes that she and my grandfather canned from their own large garden. I always put aside some of my own canned tomatoes for those cold winter months when I want a taste of summer. If you only have store-bought tomatoes it will still taste good, but home-canned have a special sweetness that makes this soup wonderful.

2 t. olive oil	3 qts. home-canned tomatoes,
1 c. onion, chopped	or 3 28-oz. cans whole
2 T. garlic, minced	tomatoes
1 to 1-1/4 lbs. ground beef	salt and pepper to taste
chuck	16-oz. pkg. elbow macaroni,
2 c. water	uncooked

Heat oil in a large stockpot over medium heat; add onion and garlic. Cook for about 3 minutes, stirring often. Add beef; cook until browned. Do not drain. Add water, tomatoes with juice, salt and pepper; bring to a boil. Reduce heat to low. Simmer for about 2 hours, stirring often. About 30 minutes before serving time, cook macaroni according to package directions; drain. To serve, add a big scoop of macaroni to each soup bowl; ladle soup over macaroni. Soup may be frozen; do not add macaroni until serving time. Makes 8 to 10 servings.

Clean up stovetop spills easily... no harsh chemicals needed. Cover cooked-on food spots with equal parts water and baking soda. Spills will soak right off.

Tom's Delicious Potato Soup

Thomas Hiegel
Union City, OH

I like potato soup, but I don't care to use milk if I can help it. So I thought I would try to make some without milk and this is what I came up with. Everyone says it is the best potato soup they have ever had...I know I sure like it!

4 potatoes, peeled and cubed
2 carrots, peeled and chopped
1 turnip, peeled and cubed
2-1/2 T. butter, sliced
2 stalks celery, chopped
1 onion, finely chopped
2-1/2 T. all-purpose flour

5 c. chicken broth
2 cubes chicken bouillon
1 T. fresh parsley, chopped
1 t. celery seed
1/2 t. salt
1/8 t. white pepper

Place potatoes, carrots and turnip in a large saucepan; cover with water. Bring to a boil over high heat. Boil for 8 minutes; drain. Add butter, celery and onion. Cook for 2 minutes, stirring occasionally. Sprinkle flour over vegetables; mix well and cook for one minute. Add broth, bouillon cubes, parsley and seasonings. Stirring constantly, bring to a boil over high heat. Reduce heat to low; cover and simmer gently for 40 minutes, or until vegetables are tender. Uncover and cook until liquid is reduced. Season with more salt and pepper, if desired. Makes 6 servings.

Don't toss out the leaves from fresh celery...they're full of flavor! Lay them on a paper towel where they'll dry in just a day or two. Store the dried leaves in a canning jar to toss into soups and stews.

Potato-Bacon Chowder

Angela Dagenbach
Harrison, OH

When my husband had surgery, our dear friend Debbie brought my family a pot of this soup. She made several different soups for my family over a period of time. This chowder was our favorite...I always say the soup nursed him back to health. We were so grateful for this showing of love.

2 c. potatoes, peeled and cubed
1 c. onion, chopped
1 c. water
8 slices bacon
10-3/4 oz. can cream of chicken
   soup

1 c. sour cream
2 c. milk
1/2 t. salt
1/8 t. pepper

In a large saucepan over medium heat, cook potatoes and onion in water until tender, 10 to 15 minutes. Do not drain. Meanwhile, in a large skillet over medium heat, cook bacon until crisp; drain and set aside. In a bowl, whisk together soup, sour cream and milk. Add soup mixture to potato mixture along with crumbled bacon, salt and pepper. Heat through over low heat; do not boil. Makes 6 servings.

Can't remember if you've already tried a recipe? Next time,
draw a little smiley face in the page's margin...
you'll remember that it was a hit!

Chicken Tortilla Soup

Jenita Davison
La Plata, MO

We love this soup! There's nothing easier than opening some cans and stirring it all together. When this soup was served at a church meeting, we all wanted the recipe. We each alter it a bit to our individual tastes...that's the wonderful thing about home cooking.

15-1/2 oz. can light red kidney beans
15-1/2 oz. can chili beans
15-1/2 oz. can hominy
15-oz. can corn
14-1/2 oz. can diced tomatoes with green chiles or Mexican diced tomatoes
14-1/2 oz. can petite diced tomatoes
1-1/4 oz. pkg. taco seasoning mix
1-oz. pkg. ranch salad dressing mix
2 boneless, skinless chicken breasts, cooked and shredded, or 10-oz. can chicken, flaked
1 green onion, diced
3/4 t. garlic, minced
catsup to taste
Garnish: tortilla chips, favorite shredded cheese

In a large soup pot over medium heat, combine all canned vegetables without draining. Add remaining ingredients except garnish; mix well. Bring to a boil. Reduce heat to low and simmer, stirring often, for about 30 minutes. May also be prepared in a 6-quart slow cooker; cover and cook on low setting for 4 to 5 hours. At serving time, ladle into soup bowls; crumble tortilla chips over top and sprinkle with cheese. Makes 10 servings.

A rainy-day cure-all...toss together ingredients for a tasty slow-cooker meal, pop some popcorn and enjoy a family movie marathon. When you're ready for dinner, it's ready for you!

Soups & Breads
to Warm the Heart

Marlene's Cornbread

Bethi Hendrickson
Danville, PA

Whenever I make this cornbread I remember Fort Bragg, North Carolina and our wonderful neighbor Marlene, a sweet southern lady who shared this family recipe with me. So good with soup and chili, or just with butter and honey as a snack.

1-1/2 c. yellow cornmeal
1/2 c. all-purpose flour
1 T. sugar
2 t. baking powder
1/2 t. baking soda

1/4 c. shortening or bacon
   drippings
1-1/2 c. buttermilk
2 eggs, beaten

Mix all ingredients in a bowl; beat vigorously for 30 seconds. Pour batter into a greased 9" cast-iron skillet or round cake pan. Bake at 450 degrees until golden, 25 to 30 minutes. Cut into wedges; serve warm. Makes 8 to 10 servings.

Mom's Chicken Noodle Cheese Soup

Angela Thurmon
Norphlet, AR

My mom came up with this simple recipe one day from items she had in the pantry. It's so good when it's cold outside and always reminds me of her.

2 chicken breasts
2-1/2 c. wide egg noodles,
   uncooked
10-3/4 oz. can cream of chicken
   soup
16-oz. can corn, drained

10-oz. can diced tomatoes and
   green chiles
1-1/2 to 2 c. shredded Cheddar
   cheese
salt and pepper to taste

Cover chicken with water in a large saucepan over medium heat. Bring to a boil; reduce heat to low and simmer until chicken is very tender. Set aside chicken, reserving broth in pan. Add noodles to broth and cook according to package directions; do not drain. Shred chicken and add to broth along with remaining ingredients. Cook and stir over low heat until bubbly and cheese is melted. Makes 4 servings.

Grammy's Chilly-Day Chili

Laurie Anderson
Mount Prospect, IL

As a child, this was my favorite winter supper. Through the years I've tweaked my mom's recipe to make it my own. It is guaranteed to have your family asking for more. It's soooo good!

2 to 3 lbs. ground beef
1 yellow onion, sliced
2 green peppers, chopped
5 14-1/2 oz. cans diced
   tomatoes
15-1/2 oz. can light red kidney
   beans
2 large or 4 small bay leaves

3 to 4 T. chili powder
1/4 t. cayenne pepper
1/4 t. paprika
1 T. salt
1/8 t. pepper
Optional: cooked elbow
   macaroni, shredded Cheddar
   cheese

In a large stockpot, brown beef over medium heat until no longer pink; drain. Add onion and pepper; cover and cook until onion is translucent and pepper is tender, about 8 minutes. Stir in undrained tomatoes. Add undrained beans and remaining ingredients; stir well. Reduce to low heat. Cover and simmer for 2 hours, stirring occasionally. At serving time, discard bay leaves; add toppings as desired. Makes 8 servings.

A great way to use leftover canned pumpkin...stir a big spoonful into a pot of spicy chili. The pumpkin adds healthy fiber without really changing the flavor of the chili.

Jalapeño Cheddar Cornbread

Jessica Kraus
Delaware, OH

My version of a southern classic that's perfect with chili!
You can adjust the jalapeños to your family's taste.

8-1/2 oz. pkg. corn muffin mix
1/4 c. butter, melted and cooled
   slightly
1 egg, beaten
1/3 c. milk

1/4 c. pickled jalapeños, diced
2 T. fresh chives, chopped
2 c. shredded Cheddar cheese,
   divided
3 T. honey

In a large bowl, combine muffin mix, melted butter, egg, milk, jalapeños, chives and 1-1/2 cups cheese. Stir well until moistened. Spoon batter into a greased 8"x8" baking pan. Drizzle honey over top; do not mix in. Top with remaining cheese. Bake at 375 degrees for 30 minutes, or until golden. Cut into squares; serve warm. Makes 8 servings.

A quick substitution for a box of corn muffin mix! Just combine 1-1/4 cups yellow cornmeal, one cup all-purpose flour, 1/2 cup sugar, 4 teaspoons baking powder and 1/2 teaspoon salt.

Roasted Tomato Bisque

Jessica Kraus
Delaware, OH

Perfect for a cold day...this luscious soup will warm you right up!
Roasting vegetables completely transforms their flavor.

3 lbs. roma tomatoes, halved
2 onions, cut into large chunks
6 cloves garlic
1/4 c. olive oil
salt and pepper to taste

28-oz. can diced tomatoes
4 c. chicken broth
1/4 t. red pepper flakes
2 c. fresh basil, chopped
1 c. whipping cream

On a large baking sheet, toss roma tomatoes, onions and garlic with oil. Season with salt and pepper. Bake at 400 degrees for 45 minutes. Meanwhile, in a large stockpot, combine undrained diced tomatoes, broth, red pepper flakes and basil; season with more salt and pepper. Simmer over low heat for about 15 minutes. Add roasted vegetables to stockpot. Simmer, uncovered, for about 30 minutes. With an immersion blender or regular blender, blend until smooth. Transfer back to pot. Add cream; heat through without boiling. Makes 8 servings.

Waffle Iron Grilled Cheese

Kathy Grashoff
Fort Wayne, IN

You'll love the gooey cheese and the dimples from the waffle iron!
Add a bowl of hot soup and you have a quick busy-day meal.

1 T. butter, softened
2 slices sandwich bread

3/4 c. shredded fontina,
    Muenster or Cheddar cheese

Spread butter over one side of each bread slice. Place one bread slice on a heated waffle iron, butter-side down. Top with cheese and second bread slice, butter-side up. Close waffle iron; cook for about 2 minutes until golden. Makes one sandwich.

Loaded Leek Soup

Courtney Stultz
Columbus, KS

When I was growing up, my mother often made a potato-onion soup because it was fast, cheap and tasted good. I wanted to recreate this soup with extra flavor but also a little lighter on calories.

10 c. chicken or vegetable broth
1/2 head cauliflower, chopped
2 turnips, peeled and diced
2 potatoes, peeled and diced
2 leeks, finely diced

1 t. ground sage
2 t. sea salt
1 t. pepper
Optional: additional diced
    leek greens

In a large stockpot, combine all ingredients except optional garnish. Bring to a boil over high heat. Reduce heat to medium-low. Cover and cook until vegetables are soft, stirring occasionally, about 45 minutes. May also be prepared in a 6-quart slow cooker; cover and cook on high setting for 4 hours, or low setting for 8 hours. Blend lightly using an immersion blender, leaving some texture to vegetables. Garnish with additional leek greens, if desired. Makes 8 servings.

Leeks are delicious, but are often sandy when purchased.
To quickly clean them, slice into 2-inch lengths and soak in
a bowl of cold water. Swish them in the water and drain.
Refill the bowl and swish again until the water is clear.
Drain, pat dry and they're ready to use.

Ham & Bean Soup

Aubrey Nygren
Farmington, NM

I grew up eating this soup and now...each time I make it, so many memories from my childhood come with it. My Marmy used to make it by soaking the beans overnight. Now we speed up the process a bit by using canned beans and a slow cooker. I've spiced it up by adding green chiles. Serve with hot cornbread or rolls.

4 15-oz. cans pinto beans
1 onion, diced
Optional: 1 to 2 4-oz. cans
   diced green chiles

granulated garlic, salt and
   pepper to taste
1 ham hock or 1 c. cooked ham,
   cubed

In a 6-quart slow cooker, combine undrained beans, onion and green chiles, if using. Stir to combine. Add seasonings to taste; stir again. Add ham hock or cubed ham. Cover and cook on low setting for 5 to 6 hours. If using a ham hock, remove and dice ham; return ham to soup before serving. Makes 6 servings.

A quick & easy way to thicken bean soup! Purée a cup of soup
in a blender or even mash it in a bowl, then stir it
back into the soup pot.

No-Knead Scrumptious Bread

Janis Parr
Ontario, Canada

*This easy yeast bread makes three golden loaves to enjoy or share.
The smell of fresh bread baking takes me right back to my
childhood days. These loaves freeze well.*

2-3/4 c. warm water
2 envs. quick-rising dry yeast
2 t. salt, divided
2 c. plus 1 t. all-purpose flour,
   divided

2 c. all-purpose flour, divided
3 eggs, well beaten
1/2 c. sugar
1/2 c. oil
1/2 c. butter, melted

Heat water until very warm, about 110 to 115 degrees. In a small
bowl, mix yeast, 3/4 cup warm water, one teaspoon salt and
one teaspoon flour; set aside. In a large bowl, combine remaining
flour, remaining water, remaining salt, eggs, sugar and oil. Add yeast
mixture; stir well until dough forms. Let stand, uncovered, for 3 hours,
stirring occasionally. Shape dough into 3 loaves and place in 3 greased
9"x5" loaf pans. Let rise in a warm place for one hour. Brush tops with
melted butter. Bake at 350 degrees for 55 minutes, or until loaves are
golden and sound hollow when tapped with a knife. Immediately
remove loaves from pans; cool on a wire rack. Makes 3 loaves.

Scrumptious herb butter makes warm fresh-baked bread
taste even better. Blend 1/2 cup softened butter with a teaspoon
each of chopped fresh parsley, dill and chives. Roll into
a log or pack into a crock.

White Bean Soup with Salsa

Paulette Alexander
Newfoundland, Canada

I wasn't too sure about this recipe the first time I made it. But it turned out great...my son and I love it! It's definitely a wholesome meal the entire family will love.

1-1/2 c. dried white kidney
  beans or navy beans
2 t. olive oil
1 onion, diced
3 cloves garlic, minced
1 t. red pepper flakes
8 c. chicken broth
2 to 3 T. salsa

1/2 c. elbow macaroni, uncooked
1/2 t. garlic powder
1/2 t. onion powder
1/2 t. turmeric
1/2 t. dried marjoram
1/2 t. pepper
Optional: additional salsa

Place beans in a large bowl; cover generously with water. Cover bowl; let soak for 3 hours at room temperature or refrigerate overnight. Drain beans and rinse well; set aside. Heat oil in a stockpot over medium heat. Add onion, garlic and red pepper flakes; cook and stir until softened and golden. Add drained beans and broth to saucepan; bring to a boil over high heat. Reduce heat to low. Cover and simmer for about one hour, or until beans are tender, stirring occasionally. Stir in salsa. Add soup to a blender, 1/2 cup at a time. Partially cover blender and process until puréed; return to saucepan. If desired, thin soup with additional broth or water. Stir in uncooked macaroni and seasonings; cook for 10 minutes, until tender. If desired, top individual soup bowls with a spoonful of salsa. Serves 6.

Tuck bay leaves, sprigs of fresh herbs and whole peppercorns into a mesh tea ball that can hang on the side of the soup pot... easy to remove when done.

Italian Meatball Stew

Susan Reinke
Conneaut, OH

My mother always made this hearty stew when the green beans were ready to be picked from the garden. Serve with warm, buttered slices of Italian bread for a wonderful, satisfying meal.

1-1/2 lbs. ground beef round
1 c. seasoned dry bread crumbs
1/2 c. grated Parmesan cheese
salt and pepper to taste
28-oz. can Italian tomato sauce
3-1/2 c. water
dried oregano to taste

8 to 10 potatoes, peeled and
   cubed
3 to 4 c. fresh green beans,
   trimmed and cut into
   bite-size pieces
Garnish: grated Parmesan
   cheese

Combine beef, bread crumbs, Parmesan cheese, salt and pepper in a large bowl. Mix well with your hands; form into nickel-size meatballs. Add meatballs to a large skillet over medium heat; brown on all sides. Drain; transfer meatballs to a large soup pot. Add sauce, water and oregano. Bring to a boil; reduce heat to low. Cover and simmer for 30 minutes, stirring occasionally. Season with additional salt and pepper. Add potatoes and beans; return to a boil over medium-high heat. Reduce heat to medium-low; cook for another 20 minutes, or until potatoes are tender. Garnish individual servings with Parmesan cheese. Makes 6 to 8 servings.

Wondering how to safely season raw ground beef to taste?
Mix in the seasonings, then just pinch off a small sample
patty and brown it in a small skillet.

Down-Home Buttermilk Biscuits

Beckie Apple
Grannis, AR

These biscuits just beg to be spread with soft butter. They are delicious with a spoonful of your favorite jam tucked inside! My mother taught me to make biscuits when I was ten years old. I have learned over the years that two things are important in making a good biscuit, buttermilk and practice.

2-1/2 c. self-rising flour, divided
1 T. baking powder
1 t. sugar
3 T. cold butter, chipped

1 c. buttermilk
2 T. mayonnaise
1 T. water

In a bowl, combine 2 cups flour, baking powder and sugar; mix well. Add butter; use your fingers to crumble butter into flour mixture to form a coarse, mealy texture. Add buttermilk, mayonnaise and water. Stir until well blended. Sprinkle work surface with remaining flour. Gently knead dough 3 to 4 times; form into a log about 3 inches in diameter. Keeping hands well-floured, pinch off 12 equal sections of dough; roll into balls. Place biscuits in a generously oiled 8"x8" baking pan. Turn each biscuit over to coat both sides with oil. Bake at 400 degrees for 20 to 25 minutes, until golden on top and bottom. Makes one dozen.

Make a flavorful salad dressing with leftover buttermilk. Combine 1/2 cup buttermilk, 1/2 cup mayonnaise, one teaspoon dried parsley, 1/2 teaspoon onion powder, 1/4 teaspoon garlic powder, 1/8 teaspoon dill weed and a little salt and pepper.
Keep refrigerated.

Grandma Jo's Brown Bread

Barbara Ann
Fairbury, IL

Grandma often baked this bread for us when we
were spending summers with her back east.

1 c. all-purpose flour
1 c. whole-wheat flour
1/2 t. salt
1 c. buttermilk
1 t. baking soda
1/2 c. brown sugar, packed

3 T. molasses
1 T. shortening, melted
3/4 to 1 c. water
Optional: 1 c. raisins and/or
    1 c. chopped walnuts

In a large bowl, combine flours and salt; mix well. Add buttermilk, baking soda, brown sugar and molasses. Add shortening and enough water to make a thin batter. Do not overmix. Fold in raisins and/or nuts, if desired. Pour batter into a greased 9"x5" loaf pan. Bake at 375 degrees for 45 minutes. Turn loaf out of pan; cool on a wire rack for 30 minutes before slicing. Makes one loaf.

Bake up little mini loaves of bread...they're fun to eat and make great gifts. Grease soup cans well and spoon in batter, filling a bit more than 1/2 full. Set cans on a baking sheet and bake at 350 degrees for 25 to 30 minutes.

Hot & Cold Stromboli

Jessica Branch
Colchester, IL

This is one of my hubby's favorites. I like it hot out of the oven and he likes it cold the day after. We munch on this for dinner, snacks or supper. It's also a tasty take-along treat...just pack it in a cooler.

2 loaves frozen bread dough
1/2 lb. deli ham, thinly sliced
1/2 lb. deli salami, thinly sliced
1/2 lb. deli bologna, thinly sliced
1/2 lb. Swiss cheese, thinly
   sliced
1/2 c. green pepper, diced

1/2 c. onion, diced
1/4 c. black olives, sliced
1/4 c. green olives, sliced
1/2 t. garlic salt
1/2 t. Italian seasoning
2 T. olive oil

Line a 15"x10" jelly-roll pan with parchment paper; spray with non-stick vegetable spray. Place both frozen loaves end-to-end on pan; thaw according to package directions. When thawed, roll out both loaves together to cover the pan. Layer meats and cheese over dough; scatter green pepper, onion and olives over cheese. Sprinkle with seasonings. Roll up layered dough jelly-roll style; place seam-side down on pan. Let rise for one hour. Drizzle olive oil over rolled dough. Bake at 400 degrees for 15 minutes. Reduce oven temperature to 350 degrees; bake an additional 15 minutes. Slice and serve hot or cold. Serves 8.

Antipasto salad-on-a-stick is a fun side for sandwiches! On skewers, arrange cherry tomatoes, cubes of mozzarella cheese, artichoke hearts and ripe olives. Drizzle with Italian dressing and serve.

Hot Ham & Cheese Pull-Apart Loaf

Nola Coons
Gooseberry Patch

This was always my mother's go-to recipe whenever she knew my brother was bringing home his buddies after school. It's still a family favorite!

12-inch loaf Italian bread
3 T. butter, softened
1 T. spicy brown mustard

6 slices Swiss cheese
3/4 lb. deli ham, thinly sliced

With a serrated knife, cut bread into 12 slices, 3/4-inch thick, cutting to within 1/4 inch of bottom. Do not cut through loaf. Blend butter and mustard in a cup. Spread 2 teaspoons butter mixture between each pair of slices, creating 6 sandwiches. Cut cheese slices in half diagonally to form triangles. Insert 2 cheese triangles into each sandwich. Divide ham evenly among sandwiches, tucking in to fit. Spray a large sheet of heavy-duty aluminum foil with non-stick vegetable spray. Place loaf in center of foil; wrap and tightly seal foil. Place foil package on a baking sheet. Bake at 350 degrees for 40 to 45 minutes, until heated through and cheese is melted. To serve, open foil carefully to allow steam to escape. Pull apart sandwiches; serve hot. Makes 6 sandwiches.

Pick up a stack of retro-style plastic burger baskets. Lined with paper napkins, they're such fun for serving sandwiches with a side of potato chips or crisp veggies.

Saturday Sandwiches

Claire Martin
Salina, KS

My mother often made these tasty open-faced sandwiches on Saturday nights after a pleasant day working around the house and yard. We enjoyed them with baked beans and potato chips. They made Saturday evenings fun and festive.

16 slices deli ham
6 T. butter, softened and divided
4 hoagie rolls, split and
   separated

mayonnaise to taste
8 canned pineapple rings,
   cut in half
8 slices Swiss cheese

Heat a skillet over medium heat. Working in batches, cook ham in butter until golden, using 4 ham slices and 2 teaspoons butter at a time. Remove cooked ham to a plate. Meanwhile, separate each roll into 2 halves; arrange cut-side up on a baking sheet. Spread each half-roll with 1-1/2 teaspoons butter. Bake at 450 degrees for about 5 minutes, until lightly toasted. Remove from oven; spread each half-roll lightly with mayonnaise. Top each with 2 slices ham, 2 pineapple ring halves and one cheese slice. Turn oven to broil; broil sandwiches until cheese is bubbly. Serves 4, 2 open-faced sandwiches each.

Invite everyone to a soup & sandwich party...perfect for game day! With a big pot of your heartiest soup or chili simmering on the stove, freshly made grilled cheese sandwiches and brownies for dessert, you'll all have time to relax and enjoy the game.

Hoagie Hamburger Boats

Kisha Landeros
Pacific, MO

This is a dish my brother and I would always request! My mom made these sandwiches for us for busy afternoons and school nights. Simple to make, very filling and easy clean-up.

6 hoagie rolls
1 to 1-1/2 lbs. ground beef
10-3/4 oz. can cream of
   mushroom soup

salt and pepper to taste
6 slices American cheese

Slice off the tops of hoagie rolls. Pull out the centers of rolls to create "boats." Set aside tops and bread pieces. In a skillet over medium heat, brown beef; drain. Stir in soup and bread pieces; season with salt and pepper. Simmer for a few minutes, until heated through. Place rolls on a baking sheet; spoon beef mixture into rolls. Add cheese slices; replace tops onto rolls. Bake at 400 degrees for 10 to 15 minutes, until cheese is melted. Makes 6 servings.

Pickles are a must with sandwiches...don't toss that almost-empty pickle jar! Make tangy marinated veggies in a jiffy. Add cut-up cucumbers, green peppers, carrots, cauliflower and other favorite fresh veggies to the remaining pickle juice. Refrigerate and enjoy within a few days.

Nana's Southwest Beef Sandwich
Becky Smith
Maryville, MT

I enjoyed a sandwich similar to this at a local coffee shop and thought it was worth trying at home. My family agreed! They frequently ask for these sandwiches, and my grandson always requests them for his special birthday dinner.

1 t. olive or canola oil
2 to 3 thin slices onion,
   separated into rings
2 to 3 thin slices green pepper
2 slices sourdough bread

chipotle mayonnaise to taste
2 slices Pepper Jack cheese
1/4 lb. deli roast beef, thinly
   sliced
2 to 3 t. margarine, softened

Heat oil in a skillet over medium heat; add onion and green pepper. Cook, stirring frequently, until onion is soft, golden and caramelized. Spread one side of each bread slice with mayonnaise; top each with a cheese slice. Arrange beef on one cheese slice; spoon onion mixture over other cheese slice. Close sandwich; spread margarine on both sides of sandwich. In same skillet over medium heat, cook sandwich on both sides until golden and cheese is melted. Makes one sandwich.

Microwave raw onions on high in a covered container for one to two minutes before peeling and slicing. They'll lose some of the "hot" taste...helpful to know when you're serving them uncooked on sandwiches or in salads.

BBQ Chicken Melts

Melissa Dattoli
Richmond, VA

A tasty, quick dinner that can be prepared on the grill or in the oven. We like these sandwich-style, but you can serve the chicken without the buns if you prefer.

4 boneless, skinless chicken breasts
1/2 c. barbecue sauce, divided
4 slices deli ham

4 slices provolone cheese
4 hamburger buns, split
Optional: mayonnaise to taste

Brush chicken breasts with half of the barbecue sauce. Place on a hot grill; cook on both sides until chicken juices run clear. May also be placed in a greased baking pan. Bake, uncovered, at 450 degrees for 20 to 25 minutes, turning once, until done. Brush chicken with remaining barbecue sauce. Top each with a slice of ham and a slice of cheese. Grill or bake just until cheese is melted. Serve on buns with a little mayonnaise, if desired. Makes 4 sandwiches.

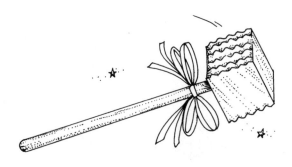

Boneless chicken breasts cook up quickly and evenly when flattened. Simply place chicken between two pieces of plastic wrap and gently pound to desired thickness with a meat mallet or a small skillet.

Tomato Sandwiches with Olive Mayonnaise

Gladys Kielar
Whitehouse, OH

So delicious any time of year...especially good made with sun-ripened tomatoes in summer.

2 T. olive oil
1 t. red wine vinegar
1 clove garlic, minced
1/2 c. fresh parsley, chopped
1/4 t. pepper
2 to 3 ripe beefsteak tomatoes,
    sliced

6 T. mayonnaise
7 black olives, minced
12 slices sourdough bread,
    lightly toasted
6 large lettuce leaves

In a large bowl, whisk together oil, vinegar and garlic. Stir in parsley and pepper. Add tomato slices; turn gently to coat and let stand for 30 minutes. In a small bowl, stir together mayonnaise and olives. Spread mixture over 6 bread slices. Arrange tomato slices on top; drizzle with any marinade remaining in bowl. Top each with a lettuce leaf; add remaining bread slices. Makes 6 sandwiches.

Treat the family to a fresh pitcher of old-fashioned lemonade! Combine 1/2 cup water and 1/2 cup sugar in a small saucepan. Bring to a boil; cook and stir until sugar dissolves; cool. Combine the sugar syrup, the juice of 6 lemons and 3 cups water in a pitcher. Chill and serve.

Romaine Chicken Caesar Wraps

Sue Klapper
Muskego, WI

*We love this tasty sandwich! It's simple to fix...perfect when
we all arrive home hungry for a quick bite.*

2 romaine lettuce hearts,
  chopped into bite-size pieces
2 c. cooked chicken, cubed
1 c. shredded Parmesan cheese
1/4 c. red onion, thinly sliced
1 c. creamy Caesar salad
  dressing

8 9-inch flavored or plain flour
  tortillas
Optional: additional salad
  dressing

Place lettuce in a large bowl. Add chicken, cheese, onion and salad
dressing; toss well to coat and set aside. Soften tortillas in microwave
oven, about 20 seconds on high. To make wraps, place each tortilla
on a plate and spoon salad mixture along the center. Drizzle with
additional dressing, if desired. Roll up tortilla from one side,
burrito-style; fold the bottom up and in to hold the salad.
Makes 8 sandwiches.

A savory roast chicken from the deli is the busy cook's secret
ingredient! The chicken is already cooked and ready for whatever
recipe you decide to make...just slice, chop or shred as needed.

Egg Salad Sandwiches

Gladys Kielar
Whitehouse, OH

For years, we have made these little finger sandwiches for family get-togethers. They always disappear quickly.

5 to 6 eggs, hard-boiled, peeled
    and grated
2 T. sweet pickle relish
2 T. mayonnaise
1 T. sour cream
1/2 t. Dijon mustard

1/4 t. sugar
1/4 t. salt
1/3 t. pepper
20 thin slices white sandwich
    bread

In a bowl, combine all ingredients except bread. Mix well; cover and chill for 3 hours. Spread 2 tablespoons of egg mixture evenly on one side of 10 bread slices. Top with remaining bread slices. Cut each sandwich into 4 thin "fingers." Makes 40 small sandwiches.

Eggs are a great source of protein! Fresh eggs can safely be refrigerated for 4 to 5 weeks, so stock up when they're on sale. Store eggs in their cartons, preferably in the coldest part of the fridge.

Garden-Fresh
Sides & Salads

Squash Medley

Christy Young
North Attleboro, MA

A fresh, tasty side that's easy to make. This goes well with just about anything...it can even be served over pasta.

1 T. olive oil
1 clove garlic, minced
1 yellow squash, sliced
1 zucchini, sliced
1 plum tomato, chopped

Optional: 1/2 c. sliced
    mushrooms
1 t. dried basil
Garnish: grated Parmesan
    cheese

Heat oil with garlic in saucepan over medium heat. Add vegetables and basil. Cook for 10 to 15 minutes, stirring occasionally, to desired tenderness. Remove from heat; sprinkle with Parmesan cheese. Makes 4 servings.

Headed for the farmers' market? Sew up a quick shopping tote with snips of farmhouse calicos and other vintage fabrics. It'll be so handy for carrying home your goodies!

Sides & Salads

Gingered Broccoli

Joan Thamsen
Middletown, NY

*Our family has enjoyed this recipe every holiday for many years.
Typically we serve it with the roast beef on Christmas Day.
Easy and elegant for any table!*

2 t. olive oil
2 T. fresh ginger, peeled and
   grated
3 cloves garlic, chopped

1 lb. fresh or frozen broccoli
   flowerets
3 T. soy sauce

Heat oil in a skillet over medium heat. Add ginger and garlic; sauté for
one to 2 minutes. Add broccoli; cook to desired tenderness. Add soy
sauce; cook over low heat for several more minutes to allow flavors to
blend. Serve immediately. Makes 6 servings.

Cheesy Broccoli-Rice Bake

Jennie Gist
Gooseberry Patch

A tasty potluck favorite, changed up with fresh broccoli.

1 bunch fresh broccoli, cut into
   flowerets
1/4 c. celery, chopped
1/4 c. onion, diced
2 t. olive oil
2 c. cooked rice

1-1/2 c. shredded Colby cheese,
   divided 10-3/4 oz. can cream
   of celery soup
3/4 c. milk
salt and pepper to taste

Cover broccoli with water in a saucepan. Cook over medium heat just
until tender; drain. In a small skillet over medium heat, sauté celery
and onion in oil. In a greased 2-quart casserole, combine broccoli,
celery mixture, rice, seasonings and one cup cheese. Whisk together
soup and milk; pour over top and mix gently. Sprinkle remaining
cheese on top. Bake, covered, at 350 degrees for 25 to 35 minutes,
until hot and bubbly. Serves 6.

Green Beans in Hot Vinaigrette

Janet Myers
Reading, PA

When my mother went on a cholesterol-free diet 20 years ago, she began using this recipe. It is liked by everyone and a favorite at special family dinners. To save time, I often prepare and refrigerate the vinaigrette mixture in advance.

3/4 lb. fresh green beans, trimmed	1 T. red wine vinegar
	1 t. Dijon mustard
1/3 c. green onions, chopped	3 T. olive oil
2 t. fresh parsley, snipped	salt and pepper to taste
2 T. cloves garlic, minced	

Place beans and onions in a saucepan; add a small amount of water. Cook over medium heat for 5 to 6 minutes, until crisp-tender. Drain vegetables well and return to saucepan. In a bowl, combine parsley, garlic, vinegar and mustard. Gradually whisk in oil. Season with salt and pepper; stir until well blended. Pour sauce over vegetables in saucepan; heat through over low heat. Makes 6 servings.

It's easy to save leftover fresh herbs. Spoon chopped herbs into an ice cube tray, one tablespoon per cube. Cover with water and freeze. Frozen cubes can be dropped right into hot dishes as they cook.

Sides & Salads

Mom's Fresh Red Beets

Joan White
Malvern, PA

I enjoy preparing this recipe because it gives me a chance to use the fresh beets from our garden. It's so good, and very colorful!

4 c. beets, peeled and sliced
3/4 c. sugar
2 t. cornstarch
1/3 c. vinegar
3 T. butter, sliced

1 t. dry mustard
1 t. onion powder
1/4 t. salt
1/8 t. white pepper

In a large saucepan, cover beets with water. Cook over medium heat until tender, about 15 minutes. Drain beets, reserving 1/3 cup cooking liquid. In same saucepan, combine sugar and cornstarch. Add reserved liquid and vinegar; stir well and bring to a boil. Add beets, butter and seasonings; reduce heat to low. Heat through. Serves 6 to 8.

Sunshine Glazed Carrots

Sue Klapper
Muskego, WI

I enjoy this light, citrusy change from the usual brown sugar glaze.

5 carrots, peeled and cut
    diagonally in 1-inch pieces
1 T. sugar
1 T. cornstarch

1/4 t. ginger
1/4 t. salt
1/4 c. orange juice
2 T. butter, sliced

In a saucepan, cover carrots with water. Cook over medium heat just until tender, about 15 minutes; drain and place in a covered serving bowl. Meanwhile, in a small saucepan, combine sugar, cornstarch and seasonings. Add orange juice; cook, stirring constantly, until thickened. Stir in butter. Pour over hot carrots; toss to coat evenly. Serve hot. Makes 4 servings.

Roasted Broccoli & Tomato Noodles

Andrea Gast
O'Fallon, MO

My husband and I eat this dish weekly. It fills us up, and we feel so healthy afterwards! It is a great way to use up all those grape tomatoes from our garden too.

16-oz. pkg. medium egg
  noodles, uncooked
1 bunch broccoli, cut into
  bite-size flowerets
20 grape tomatoes
3 cloves garlic, minced

2 T. olive oil
1 T. red pepper flakes
salt and pepper to taste
Garnish: shredded Parmesan
  cheese

Cook noodles according to package directions; drain. Meanwhile, place broccoli, tomatoes and garlic on a rimmed baking sheet. Drizzle with olive oil; toss to coat well. Sprinkle with seasonings. Bake at 400 degrees for 20 minutes, or until broccoli is tender and golden. To serve, top cooked noodles with roasted broccoli mixture and Parmesan cheese. Makes 6 servings.

Aged Parmesan cheese is most flavorful when it's freshly grated. To keep it fresh in the fridge for several weeks, wrap a chunk of Parmesan in a paper towel dampened with cider vinegar and then tuck it into a plastic zipping bag.

Country Corner Macaroni & Tomatoes

Louise Spires
Columbia, KY

I am 85 years old. For 22 years, my husband Robert and I ran a small country store where I served home-cooked meals. This simple dish was a favorite among our regular customers.

2 c. elbow macaroni, uncooked
15-oz. can Italian-style diced
   tomatoes

15-oz. can tomato sauce
1/3 c. margarine
1/4 c. sugar

Cook macaroni according to package directions. Drain and return macaroni to saucepan. Add tomatoes with juice and remaining ingredients. Simmer over low heat until warmed through, about 20 minutes. If mixture becomes too thick, stir in a small amount of water. May be spooned into a small slow cooker set on low for serving. Makes 6 servings.

Green Chile Mac & Cheese

Trish Patterson
Colorado Springs, CO

This quick and tasty recipe came from a neighbor and it has become a family favorite. The ingredients can be kept in your pantry. Use canned green chiles of the heat level your family can tolerate!

10-3/4 oz. can Cheddar cheese
   soup
1-1/4 c. milk

1 c. elbow macaroni, uncooked
4-oz. can diced green chiles

Combine soup and milk in a saucepan over medium-high heat. Stir until smooth; add uncooked macaroni. Bring to a boil; reduce heat to medium. Simmer over medium heat for 10 to 15 minutes, until macaroni is tender, stirring often to avoid burning. Stir in undrained chiles; heat through. Serves 4.

Aunt Ted's Hominy Casserole

Beckie Apple
Grannis, AR

My husband's Aunt Ted made a hominy casserole that the whole family loved. Unfortunately I did not get her recipe from her before she passed away. After several attempts at reproducing her recipe, I finally came up with this one that comes pretty close. We enjoy this casserole with hot buttered cornbread.

1/2 lb. ground pork breakfast
   sausage
1/2 c. onion, diced
1/2 c. green pepper, diced
10-3/4 oz. can cream of
   mushroom soup
1/2 t. garlic powder

1/2 t. salt
1/2 t. pepper
1 c. shredded Cheddar cheese
2 15-oz. cans yellow hominy,
   drained
Optional: additional shredded
   Cheddar cheese

In a large skillet over medium heat, cook sausage, onion and green pepper until sausage is no longer pink. Drain; stir in soup, seasonings and cheese. Cook and stir for 2 to 3 minutes. Add hominy to sausage mixture and stir well. Transfer to a greased 2-quart casserole dish; cover with aluminum foil. Bake at 375 degrees for 20 to 30 minutes, until bubbly. If desired; top with additional cheese; return to oven just until cheese melts. Makes 6 servings.

Pick up a vintage divided serving dish or two...they're just right for serving up a choice of veggie sides without crowding the table.

Scarlett's Corn Pudding

Scarlett Hedden
Port Saint John, FL

This dish has been in my favorite recipes for quite awhile. It is low in calories, fat and cholesterol and it tastes delicious. Serve it to company and they won't even know they're eating healthy!

2 c. fat-free evaporated milk	2 t. baking powder
1-1/2 c. egg substitute	1/2 t. salt substitute
2 T. margarine, melted	6 c. fresh corn kernels,
1/4 c. all-purpose flour	or frozen corn, thawed
1/4 c. stevia powdered	and drained
sweetener	

In a large bowl, combine milk, egg substitute and margarine; set aside. In a small bowl, combine flour, stevia, baking powder and salt substitute; add to milk mixture and stir until smooth. Stir in corn. Spoon into a 13"x9" baking pan coated with non-stick vegetable spray. Bake, uncovered, at 350 degrees for 40 to 45 minutes, until set and golden. Let stand 5 minutes before serving. Makes 8 servings.

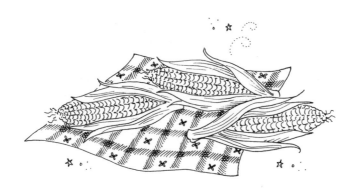

Enjoy the summery taste of fresh sweet corn year 'round. Remove husks; stack ears in a large pot and cover with water. Bring to a boil and cook for 5 minutes. Drain; chill ears in ice water until they're cool enough to handle. Cut off the kernels and store in freezer bags.

Skillet Fajita Vegetables

Sherry Sheehan
Phoenix, AZ

After I was put on an ultra low-carb diet, I looked for something that would give me the flavor of fajitas without the carbs from the flour tortillas. This recipe for a tasty side dish is what I came up with. Make it a delicious main dish by adding sliced grilled steak or chicken breast.

2 T. extra-virgin olive oil
1 onion, cut into small wedges
1 clove garlic, minced
1 green pepper, cut into strips

1 red pepper, cut into strips
1 orange or yellow pepper,
   cut into strips
1 t. ground cumin

In a large cast-iron skillet, heat oil over medium-high heat. Add onion and garlic; sauté for one to 2 minutes. Add peppers; sauté for another 5 to 6 minutes until soft, golden and caramelized, stirring occasionally. Stir in cumin; serve immediately. Makes 6 servings.

For the healthiest meals, choose from a rainbow of veggies...
red beets, orange sweet potatoes, yellow summer squash,
dark green kale and Brussels sprouts, purple eggplant and
blueberries. Fill your plate and eat up!

Cauliflower Fried Rice

Annette McDonald
Tacoma, WA

This is a fun recipe! Always counting carbs, our family loves this dish and we tweak it to fit our various tastes. Feel free to add bamboo shoots, water chestnuts, sliced celery, broccoli flowerets or other veggies. This can easily become a main dish by adding chopped cooked meat, shrimp or tofu.

1/2 t. sesame oil	1 egg, beaten
4 t. canola oil, divided	3-1/2 c. fresh cauliflower, grated
1/2 c. onion, chopped	2 T. light soy sauce
1/2 c. fresh or frozen peas or snow peas	Garnish: 2 green onions, chopped
1/2 c. mushrooms, thinly sliced	

In a large skillet, heat sesame oil and 3 teaspoons canola oil over medium-high heat. Add onion; sauté for 2 to 4 minutes. Add peas and mushrooms; cook an additional 3 to 5 minutes, stirring often. Meanwhile, in a separate small skillet over low heat, lightly scramble egg in remaining canola oil. Add cauliflower, soy sauce and scrambled egg to mixture in large skillet. Cook 5 to 8 minutes more, stirring often. Serve garnished with chopped green onions.

"Light" soy sauce is light-colored when compared to dark soy sauce, not lighter in calories or sodium. For a lower-sodium soy sauce, try diluting regular soy sauce with a little water.

Tastes Like Home

Refrigerator Mashed Potatoes

Carolyn Deckard
Bedford, IN

My daughter Sherry Lynn got this recipe from a teacher at the school where she works. She has made them for us lots of times. They are very very good!

5 lbs. potatoes, peeled and cubed
2 3-oz. pkgs. cream cheese, softened
1 c. sour cream
2 T. butter, softened
2 t. salt
1/4 t. pepper
Garnish: additional butter

Cover potatoes with water in a large saucepan. Cook over medium-high heat until fork-tender, 15 to 20 minutes. Drain and mash potatoes. Add remaining ingredients except garnish; beat until light and fluffy. Cool; cover tightly and refrigerate up to 4 days. To serve, transfer desired amount to a casserole; dot with butter. Bake, uncovered, at 350 degrees for about 30 minutes, until heated through. Serves 12.

Potato & Carrot Mash

Marilyn Donavan
Fitchburg, ME

My mother made this often when I was growing up. It was a tasty side dish for pork cutlets and meatloaf. The carrots give the mash a sweet flavor and an orangy color that we enjoy.

10 to 12 potatoes, peeled and cubed
12 carrots, peeled and sliced
1 t. salt
1/2 c. butter, softened
salt and pepper to taste

Cover potatoes and carrots with water in a large saucepan; add salt. Bring to a boil over heat; reduce heat to medium and cook until fork-tender, 15 to 20 minutes. Drain; mash with a potato masher until smooth. Stir in butter until melted; season with salt and pepper. Makes 8 to 10 servings.

Spring Potato Casserole

Lori Ritchey
Denver, PA

Green onions and a touch of garlic make this a little different from other cheesy potato casseroles. Delicious served with ham in the springtime or anytime.

32-oz. pkg. frozen shredded
   hashbrowns, thawed
10-3/4 oz. can cream of potato
   soup
1/2 c. milk

1 T. butter, melted
1 t. garlic, minced
1 c. shredded Cheddar cheese
1/2 c. green onions, sliced

In a large bowl, combine all ingredients; stir gently to mix. Spoon into a lightly greased 2-quart casserole dish. Bake, uncovered, at 350 degrees for one hour, or until bubbly and golden. Makes 4 to 6 servings.

Stock up on frozen vegetables when they go on sale. Flash-frozen soon after being harvested, they retain more nutrients than fresh produce that has traveled for several days before arriving in the grocery's produce aisle.

Skillet Scalloped Potatoes

Charlotte Fortier
Lakeside, AZ

I love scalloped potatoes, but sometimes they're just too time-consuming to make. I also wanted to cut back on the calories and fat. So, I made some changes to enjoy the taste of cheesy potatoes in a lighter dish. Sometimes I add diced ham for a quick meal.

4 potatoes, peeled and thinly
   sliced
1 onion, thinly sliced
Optional: 1 green pepper, sliced
   or diced

1/4 c. low-fat milk or water
salt and pepper to taste
1 c. favorite shredded cheese

Spray a non-stick skillet with non-stick vegetable spray. Add sliced potatoes, onion and pepper, if using. Pour milk or water over top; season with salt and pepper. Turn heat to medium-high. When steam begins to form, reduce heat to low. Cover skillet and cook for 15 to 20 minutes, until potatoes are fork-tender, adding more liquid if needed. Spread cheese over top. Cover and cook over low heat for a few more minutes, until until cheese is melted. Serves 4.

Oven-Fried Eggplant

Frances Click
Hernando Beach, FL

My family enjoys fried eggplant, but we've been making an effort to eat healthier. This recipe has less fat and tastes delicious. It's one of our favorites.

1 c. Italian-seasoned dry
   bread crumbs
1 egg

2 T. olive oil
1 eggplant, sliced 1/4-inch
   thick

Place bread crumbs in a shallow dish; whisk together egg and oil in another shallow dish. Dip eggplant slices into egg mixture; roll in bread crumbs. Place slices on an ungreased baking sheet. Bake at 375 degrees until tender and golden, about 15 to 20 minutes. May be frozen and reheated. Serves 4 to 6.

Sides & Salads

Squash Patties

Lecia Stevenson
Timberville, VA

*This is such a delicious, quick and yummy recipe! My family loves it
and requests it whenever we get fresh squash from our garden.*

2 c. yellow squash, chopped	1 t. salt
1 onion, chopped	1 t. pepper
1 egg, beaten	2 to 3 T. bacon drippings or
1/2 c. all-purpose flour	oil for frying

In a bowl, combine all ingredients except drippings or oil; mix well.
Heat drippings or oil in a skillet over medium-high heat. Drop squash
mixture into skillet by large spoonfuls. Cook on each side for 4 minutes,
or until golden. Drain on paper towels. Makes 4 to 6 servings.

Hot Deviled Okra

Linda Barker
Mount Pleasant, TN

*My grandmother used to make this recipe years ago and it was
passed on to me. She raised the vegetables in her garden.*

1 c. self-rising cornmeal	1 jalapeño pepper, seeded and
pepper to taste	chopped
1 lb. okra, cut into 1/4-inch	1/3 c. bacon drippings or oil
rings	for frying
2 green tomatoes, chopped	

Mix cornmeal and pepper in a shallow dish. Dip okra, tomatoes and
jalapeño into mixture, coating well. Heat drippings or oil in a skillet
over medium-high heat. Add vegetables to skillet and cook for several
minutes, until golden. Makes 6 to 8 servings.

Look for all kinds of delicious, nutritious fresh greens at
farmstands! Try spinach, kale, Swiss chard, bok choy,
broccoli rabe or peppery mustard greens. Wilt in a hot skillet
or simmer in broth with a little sautéed onion..

Garden-to-Table Collard Greens

Helen Adams
Mabank, TX

These collard greens will just melt in your mouth! We grow collards year 'round here, but the spring collards are the tenderest. I remember picking collards with my grandmother when I was a child...the leaves seemed so big! I also remember how good those collard greens tasted when they came out of the big pot on her woodburning stove...they still taste the same to me.

2 to 2-1/2 lbs. fresh collard
   greens, stems trimmed
3 slices bacon, chopped
1 onion, chopped

2 c. chicken broth, divided
1 c. water
salt and pepper to taste
Garnish: hot pepper sauce

Place collard greens in a large container. Cover with ice-cold water and let stand for 10 minutes. Drain; rinse collard greens and cut into strips, 3/4-inch to 1-inch wide. Set aside. In a Dutch oven over medium heat, cook bacon until crisp. Remove bacon to paper towels to drain, reserving drippings in pan. Add onion to drippings; sauté until almost clear. Add one cup broth and simmer for a few minutes, scraping up brown bits from bottom of pan. Add collard greens, remaining broth and water. Bring to a boil. Reduce heat to medium-low and cook just until collard greens are almost wilted. Stir well. Cover Dutch oven with lid; bake at 325 degrees for one hour. At serving time, Season with salt and pepper; add bacon and stir well. Serve with hot sauce on the side. Makes 8 servings.

No self-rising cornmeal in the pantry? For each cup you need, just mix 3/4 cup plus 3 tablespoons regular cornmeal, one tablespoon baking powder and 1/2 teaspoon salt.

Spicy Scalloped Potatoes

Lisa Robason
Corpus Christi, TX

These flavorful potatoes make a great partner for Mexican-style meatloaf. The Jalapeño Jack cheese really turns up the heat!

4 c. potatoes, peeled, thinly
   sliced and divided
3 T. butter, sliced
3 T. all-purpose flour
1-1/2 c. milk
1 t. salt

1/4 t. cayenne pepper, or more
   to taste
1-1/2 c. shredded Jalapeño Jack
   cheese, divided
Optional: paprika or cayenne
   pepper to taste

Arrange half of potatoes in a lightly greased 13"x9" baking pan; set aside. In a saucepan over low heat, melt butter and blend in flour. Add milk; whisk until smooth. Cook over low heat until mixture begins to boil. Remove from heat; season with salt and cayenne pepper. Stir in one cup cheese. Pour half of cheese sauce over potatoes; layer with remaining potatoes. Top with remaining cheese sauce; sprinkle with remaining cheese. Sprinkle with paprika or cayenne pepper, if desired. Bake, uncovered, at 350 degrees for one hour, or until golden and potatoes are tender. Makes 6 servings.

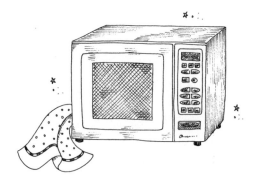

Steam crisp-tender vegetables in the microwave. Place cut-up veggies in a microwave-safe dish and add a little water. Cover with plastic wrap, venting with a knife tip. Microwave on high for 2 to 5 minutes, checking for tenderness after each minute. Uncover carefully to allow hot steam to escape.

Apple-Filled Sweet Potatoes

Hannah Hopkins
Plainfield, VT

Looking for a new way to enjoy sweet potatoes? This is a warm combination of two seasonal favorites that can be whipped up in less than an hour.

6 sweet potatoes
1/2 c. butter, softened
1/2 t. orange zest
1/8 t. nutmeg

1 c. apple, peeled, cored and
   coarsely chopped
1/4 to 1/2 c. chopped pecans
Optional: pecan halves

Pierce sweet potatoes with a fork to allow steam to escape. Bake at 375 degrees for 30 to 35 minutes, until fork-tender. Cut a thin slice lengthwise from the top of each potato. Scoop out inside, reserving potato pulp and leaving a thin shell. Place shells on a 15"x10" jelly-roll pan; set aside. In a large bowl, combine potato pulp, butter, orange zest and nutmeg. Beat with an electric mixer on medium speed, scraping bowl often, until well mixed and smooth. Stir in apple and chopped pecans with a spoon. Fill shells with sweet potato mixture. If desired, garnish each potato with pecan halves. Bake, uncovered, at 375 degrees for 15 to 20 minutes, until heated through. Makes 6 servings.

Sprinkle crumbled gingersnap cookies over sweet potato casseroles for a sweet, crunchy topping that's just a little different.

Red Rooster Sweet Potatoes

Staci Prickett
Montezuma, GA

This recipe gives a sweet heat to your sweet potatoes. You control the heat by the amount of sriracha hot sauce you use...if you don't like heat, omit the hot sauce.

2 sweet potatoes, peeled and
   cut into wedges or strips
2/3 c. brown sugar, packed
1-1/2 T. olive oil

2 t. sriracha hot chili sauce,
   or to taste
1 t. cinnamon

Place sweet potatoes in a large plastic zipping bag; set aside. Combine remaining ingredients in a cup; mix well and add to sweet potatoes. Seal bag and shake until potatoes are well coated. In a single layer, arrange potatoes on a baking sheet lightly sprayed with non-stick vegetable spray. Bake at 400 degrees for 20 minutes, or until potatoes are tender. Let cool for a few minutes before serving. Makes 4 to 6 servings.

Save time when peeling and chopping veggies. Set a large bowl on the counter to toss all the peelings into...you'll only need to make one trip to the compost bin or wastebasket.

Mom A's Cukes & Sour Cream

Nancy Erney
McIntosh, FL

*One of Mom's recipes that she could start and then
leave for me to finish while she was at work.*

2 regular cucumbers or 4 Kirby
   cucumbers, peeled and sliced
1 sweet onion, sliced
1/2 c. sour cream
2 T. white vinegar
1 T. plus 1 t. mayonnaise

1 t. seasoned salt
1/4 t. salt
1/8 t. pepper
Optional: chopped fresh or
   dried parsley

Combine cucumbers and onion in a large bowl. Place several paper
towels on top; chill in refrigerator for at least one hour. In a small bowl,
whisk together remaining ingredients except parsley. Transfer cucumber
mixture to a colander; drain excess liquid and pat dry with paper
towels. Return cucumber mixture to bowl; pour on sour cream mixture
and toss to mix. Garnish with parsley, if desired. Serve immediately,
or cover and chill until serving time. Makes 4 to 6 servings.

Look for heirloom fruits & vegetables at farmers' markets...
varieties that Grandma & Grandpa may have grown in their
garden. These fruits and veggies may not always look picture-
perfect but their time-tested flavor can't be beat!

Greek Carrot Salad

Jill Ball
Highland, UT

For some reason, I never remember to make a side dish until dinner is almost ready to serve. So I am always looking for simple sides. This one is not only quick & easy but yummy too.

3 c. carrots, peeled and
    coarsely grated
1/2 c. fresh pineapple, chopped,
    or canned pineapple tidbits,
    drained
1/4 c. raisins

1/4 c. chopped walnuts
1/2 t. cinnamon
1/2 t. ginger
1 c. vanilla yogurt or plain
    Greek yogurt

Combine all ingredients in a bowl; fold gently to mix. Serve immediately, or cover and refrigerate up to 2 days. Makes 4 to 6 servings.

Use seed packet clippings to decorate a small notebook...
oh-so handy for making shopping lists or keeping schedules.

Caprese Tomato Salad
Vickie

I love a juicy ripe summer tomato! A combo of red, yellow and orange tomatoes is pretty, if you can get them. Short on time? Cube the tomatoes and cheese, then toss all together.

3 tomatoes, sliced
1/2 lb. mozzarella cheese, sliced
1 T. fresh basil, chopped
1/4 c. olive oil
2 T. balsamic vinegar
pepper to taste

On a serving platter, arrange tomato slices in an overlapping circular pattern. Layer cheese slices between tomato slices. Sprinkle with basil; drizzle with oil and vinegar. With a fork, gently lift tomato and cheese slices to allow oil and vinegar to coat completely. Sprinkle with pepper. Let stand 15 to 30 minutes, to allow flavors to blend. Makes 6 servings.

Corn & Tomato Salad
Kathy Courington
Canton, GA

My friend Jeannie brought this salad to a potluck and I just had to have the recipe! It's become a family favorite.

3 to 4 15-oz. cans shoepeg
  corn, drained
1 to 2 tomatoes, diced and well
  drained
2 to 3 green onions, chopped
2 T. light mayonnaise

In a serving bowl, combine corn, tomatoes and onions. Add mayonnaise; stir to mix. Serve immediately, or cover and keep refrigerated. Makes 6 to 8 servings.

Keep tomatoes stored at room temperature for the best fresh-from-the-garden taste.

Peas & Thank You Salad

Sandy Bernards
Valencia, CA

*Everyone will love this salad with its funny name and
tasty mix of flavors! It's easy to double for potlucks.*

1/2 c. mayonnaise-style salad
    dressing
1/4 c. zesty Italian salad
    dressing
10-oz. pkg. frozen peas, thawed
    and drained

6 slices bacon, crisply cooked
    and crumbled
1 c. celery, chopped
1/4 c. red onion, chopped
1 c. salted peanuts

Combine salad dressings in a salad bowl; mix well. Add remaining
ingredients except peanuts; mix lightly. Cover and chill until serving
time. Just before serving, stir in peanuts. Makes 6 servings.

Do you have picky kids who won't eat veggies? Encourage
them to take a no-thank-you helping, or just one bite, of foods
they think they don't like. They may be pleasantly surprised!

Mom's Spinach Salad

Becky Smith
North Canton, OH

My mother made this delicious salad for many picnics and potlucks, and always came home with an empty bowl and lots of requests for the recipe. Now I love making it myself.

1 lb. fresh spinach, torn
2 eggs, hard-boiled, peeled and
  sliced

4 slices bacon, crumbled
grated Parmesan cheese to taste

Make Dressing ahead of time; chill. At serving time, place spinach in a large salad bowl. Top with eggs, bacon and Parmesan cheese. Pour Dressing over all; toss to mix. Makes 10 to 12 servings.

Dressing:

1/2 c. sugar
1/2 c. oil
1/3 c. catsup

1/4 c. vinegar
1 T. Worcestershire sauce
1/2 t. salt

Combine all ingredients in a shaker jar; cover and shake to mix until thoroughly blended. Refrigerate until chilled.

A fun buffet idea! Set out flatware rolled up in a napkin and tucked into a Mason jar. Handy for guests to pick up and the jar can serve as a drinking glass for lemonade or cider.

Sides & Salads

Linguine Garden Salad

Kelley Briggs
Massena, NY

I make this salad with its colorful mix of veggies every summer for family cookouts. My mother would always request it. When I make this salad it reminds me of her, and brings warm memories. A light or fat-free salad dressing may be used.

16-oz. pkg. linguine pasta, uncooked
1 English cucumber, peeled and diced
2 c. cherry or grape tomatoes

1 sweet onion, diced
1 orange or yellow pepper, diced
2 c. Cheddar cheese, cubed
3/4 c. Italian salad dressing
2 to 3 T. salad seasoning

Cook pasta according to package directions. Drain in a colander; rinse with cold water and let cool. Transfer pasta to a large serving bowl. Add vegetables and cheese; set aside. In a separate small bowl, mix together salad dressing and seasoning. Drizzle over linguine mixture; stir until well mixed. If desired, add more salad dressing and seasoning to taste. Cover and refrigerate for several hours to allow flavors to blend. Serves 8.

Try just one new herb at a time...a terrific way to learn which flavors your family likes. Some tried & true pairings are ripe tomatoes and basil, sweet corn and chives, cucumbers and mint, potatoes and rosemary.

Mom's Potato Salad

Shirley Condy
Plainview, NY

This recipe has been in the family for many years and brings back so many happy memories of my mother. Whenever I ask what to bring to picnics, the answer is always Mom's Potato Salad.

5 lbs. redskin potatoes
1 onion, chopped
1 T. oil
1 t. sugar

1/4 c. cider vinegar
salt and pepper to taste
1 c. mayonnaise, or more to
  taste

Place potatoes in a large saucepan, cutting any larger potatoes in half. Add enough water to cover. Over medium-high heat, boil potatoes until fork-tender; drain and cool. Peel potatoes and cut into cubes. In a serving bowl, combine potatoes, onion and remaining ingredients; mix well. Cover and chill until serving time. Makes 10 to 12 servings.

For potato salad, choose waxy new red, yellow or white potatoes. They'll hold their shape much better than baking potatoes when tossed with dressing.

Sides & Salads

Asparagus, Egg & Bacon Salad

Ann Mathis
Biscoe, AR

My dad planted an asparagus patch several years ago. He has since passed away, but every spring we harvest the fruits of his labor. This is one of many delicious recipes we enjoy in the spring.

1-2/3 c. fresh asparagus, trimmed and chopped
1 egg, hard-boiled, peeled and sliced

2 slices bacon, crisply cooked and crumbled

Bring a large saucepan of water to a boil over high heat. Add asparagus and cook for 2 to 3 minutes, until crisp-tender. Drain in a colander; rinse with cold water and let cool. Arrange asparagus on a serving plate. Top with egg and bacon; drizzle with Vinaigrette. Serve immediately, or cover and chill. Makes 6 servings.

Vinaigrette:

1 t. extra-virgin olive oil
1 t. red wine vinegar

1/2 t. Dijon mustard
salt and pepper to taste

In a small bowl, whisk together all ingredients.

A vintage-style salad that's ready to serve in seconds!
Top crisp wedges of iceberg lettuce with Thousand Island
salad dressing, diced tomato and bacon crumbles.

Aunt Jo's Corn Salad

Ramona Wysong
Barlow, KY

I've tried a lot of different salads over the years. My Aunt Jo made this for supper one night and we loved it. I can't eat celery so I omit it. Use regular, light or low-fat salad dressing as you prefer.

15-oz. can corn, very well
  drained
1 ripe tomato, diced, or
  1 c. canned petite diced
  tomatoes, very well drained
1/2 green pepper, diced
1/2 cucumber, peeled and diced
1/2 onion, diced
1 stalk celery, finely diced
3 T. ranch salad dressing,
  or more to taste
salt and pepper to taste

Combine all ingredients in a salad bowl and mix well. Serve at room temperature, or cover and chill for 2 hours in the refrigerator. If chilled, stir well before serving. Makes 4 servings.

Good-for-You Pasta Salad

Lee Lally
Cincinnati, OH

I received this heart-healthy recipe from a friend from a farm community. It has the best taste ever, and she made it in less than half an hour while we were talking. Best quick salad ever!

16-oz. pkg. egg-free noodles or
  whole-grain pasta, uncooked
1 c. fat-free mayonnaise
2/3 c. sugar, or calorie-free
  sweetener to taste
1/4 c. vinegar
2 T. mustard
4 ripe tomatoes, diced
Optional: 1 c. carrot, celery
  and/or green pepper,
  chopped

Cook pasta according to package directions. Drain; rinse with cold water and cool. In a large bowl, mix mayonnaise, sugar or sweetener, vinegar and mustard. Add cooked pasta, tomatoes and vegetables, if using; mix well. Cover and refrigerate for 30 minutes before serving. Makes 6 to 8 servings.

Tomato, Cucumber & Onion Salad

Liz Plotnick-Snay
Gooseberry Patch

*My husband's mother used to make this light and easy salad
and now we do too. We often substitute cherry tomatoes
that we've grown in our garden.*

6 ripe tomatoes, sliced 1/4-inch
  thick
1 onion, thinly sliced

1/2 cucumber, peeled and thinly
  sliced

Layer vegetables in a glass bowl. Pour Red Wine Dressing over
vegetables; mix gently. Let stand at room temperature for one hour
before serving. Serves 6 to 8.

Red Wine Dressing:

1 c. extra-virgin olive oil
1/3 c. red wine vinegar
1 T. fresh basil, chopped
2 t. sugar

1/2 t. dry mustard
1/2 t. garlic powder
salt to taste
1/2 t. pepper

Combine all ingredients in a small bowl; whisk well.

Inexpensive light olive oil is just fine for cooking. Save the
extra-virgin olive oil for making salad dressings,
where its delicate flavor can be enjoyed.

Molly's Un-Tater Salad

Molly Ebert
Columbus, IN

Since I was diagnosed with diabetes, I have to watch my carb intake. I tried several other recipes using cauliflower instead of potatoes but wasn't quite happy with the results. So I experimented until I finally came up with this delicious version. Even folks who think they don't like cauliflower love this!

2 16-oz. pkgs. frozen
  cauliflower, thawed
3 eggs, hard-boiled, peeled and
  diced

1/2 c. celery, sliced
1/2 c. green onions, sliced
1/2 c. dill pickles, diced
Garnish: paprika

Steam cauliflower according to package directions, just until crisp-tender. Drain; cut cauliflower into bite-size pieces and place in a large salad bowl. Add remaining ingredients except paprika. Add Dressing; toss gently to coat all ingredients. Garnish with a sprinkle of paprika. Cover and chill several hours to allow flavors to blend. Makes 12 servings.

Dressing:

1/2 c. sour cream
1/4 c. mayonnaise

1/4 c. plain Greek yogurt
1/2 t. salt

Mix together all ingredients in a small bowl.

The kitchen is the heart of the home,
and the mother is queen of the kitchen.
—Owen Meredith

Downings' Favorite Salad

Tracie Carlson
Dallas, TX

*I have been making this salad for over 35 years. I remember it being
served at many meals by my wonderful Grandma Downing when
I was a little girl. I can't recall the last time there were leftovers!*

1 head iceberg lettuce, torn
2 to 3 eggs, hard-boiled, peeled
   and diced

chopped green onions to taste

In a large salad bowl, combine lettuce, eggs and onions. Add dressing;
toss lightly. Cover and chill until serving time. Serves 8.

Dressing:

3/4 c. mayonnaise or
   mayonnaise-style salad
   dressing
3 T. sugar

1/3 c. cider vinegar or lemon
   juice
salt and lemon pepper to taste
Optional: light cream

Combine all ingredients except cream in a shaker jar. Cover and shake
together. Thin with a little cream, if desired.

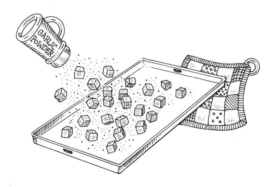

Savory homemade croutons are easy to make. Toss cubes of day-
old bread with olive oil, garlic powder, salt and pepper. Place
bread cubes in a single layer on a baking sheet and bake at
400 degrees for about 10 minutes, until toasty.

No-Mayo Cabbage Salad

Sandra Sullivan
Aurora, CO

This salad is awesome for picnics or camping! Make it several days ahead...the longer it's refrigerated, the crisper it gets.

1 head cabbage, shredded
1 onion, chopped
1 green pepper, chopped
1 c. boiling water
1 T. salt

1 c. sugar
1 c. white vinegar
1 T. celery seed
Optional: 1/2 c. carrots, peeled
 and shredded

In a large bowl, combine cabbage, onion, green pepper, boiling water and salt. Stir well; let stand for hour. Drain and add remaining ingredients; mix well. Cover and refrigerate until serving time. Salad will become crisper as it chills. Serves 6.

Apple-Cinnamon Coleslaw

Marie Warner
Jennings, FL

I love simple coleslaw combos. Adding just a touch of fruit and spice turns coleslaw into a grand side dish.

2 c. cabbage, shredded
1-1/2 c. Granny Smith apples,
 cored and chopped

1/2 c. chopped walnuts, pecans
 or almonds
1/2 c. brown or golden raisins

Combine all ingredients in a bowl; toss to mix. Pour Dressing over top; toss again. Serve immediately, or cover and refrigerate. Makes 4 to 6 servings.

Dressing:

8-oz. container vanilla yogurt
1/2 t. cinnamon

1/4 c. frozen apple juice
 concentrate, thawed

In a small bowl, combine all ingredients; blend well.

Avocado Coleslaw

Karen Fisher
Cloquet, MN

*Easy to make in a short time. If you're making it ahead of time,
add the avocado just before serving so it will be fresh and green.*

1 to 2 c. mayonnaise, to taste
1/2 c. mayonnaise-style salad
   dressing
2 T. sugar
1 T. white vinegar
1 t. celery seed
salt and pepper to taste
12-oz. pkg. shredded coleslaw
   mix

1/3 c. grape tomatoes, each cut
   into 3 to 4 pieces
1 avocado, halved, pitted and
   cubed
Optional: crisply cooked and
   crumbled bacon

In a large bowl, combine mayonnaise, salad dressing, sugar, vinegar
and seasonings; mix well. Add coleslaw mix and stir well. Fold in
tomatoes, avocado and bacon, if using. Makes 4 to 6 servings.

A quick & easy substitution when a recipe calls for crispy
crumbled bacon...try using a jar of real bacon bits instead.

Marinated Fresh Fruit Salad

Teri Lindquist
Gurnee, IL

This is my go-to salad for holidays, to bring to parties and to keep in the fridge so we have a healthy, tasty salad for meals and snacks. It is just beautiful, and the taste surprises everyone...so sweet and tangy, yet fresh and good for you. Can't beat that!

2 c. strawberries, hulled and
    halved or quartered
2 c. seedless green grapes
2 c. seedless red grapes
2 c. blueberries

2 11-oz. cans mandarin
    oranges, drained
20-oz. can pineapple chunks,
    drained and 1/4 c. juice
    reserved

Combine all fruits in a large clear glass serving bowl. Drizzle Marinade over fruit; toss gently to combine. Cover and refrigerate for several hours to overnight. Toss again before serving. Makes 10 servings.

Marinade:

1/4 c. reserved pineapple juice
1/4 c. lemon juice

1/4 c. honey

Whisk together all ingredients in a small bowl.

The bright colors of fresh fruit really shine in an antique cut-glass bowl. When washing cut glass, add a little white vinegar to the rinse water...the glass will sparkle!

Piña Colada Fruit Salad

Ramona Storm
Gardner, IL

This salad came about one day when I was trying to use up some odds & ends of fruit in my fridge. Now we enjoy it often. It's simple, fresh-tasting and easy to put together.

1/2 c. strawberries, hulled
   and quartered
1/2 c. blueberries
1/2 c. seedless grapes, halved

1/2 c. pineapple cubes
1 banana, sliced
6-oz. container piña colada
   yogurt

Combine all fruits in a bowl. Gently stir in yogurt, coating well. Cover and refrigerate for one hour before serving. Makes 4 servings.

Spoon fruit or veggie salads into mini Mason jars...
fun for a summer buffet and convenient to tuck
in a picnic basket.

Pat's Spinach Salad with Strawberries

Sandy Perry
Bakersfield, CA

My good friend Pat invited me over for a quilt lesson and made the most wonderful salad for us that hot June day. I just had to have the recipe!

6-oz. pkg. fresh spinach, torn
2 c. strawberries, hulled and
   sliced

11-oz. can mandarin oranges,
   drained
1/2 c. sliced almonds

In a large salad bowl, combine spinach, strawberries and oranges. Pour Dressing lightly over salad; toss to mix. Sprinkle almonds on top. Makes 6 to 8 servings.

Dressing:

1/2 c. olive oil
2 T. lemon juice
2 T. sugar

1 t. brown mustard
salt and pepper to taste

Combine all ingredients in a jar; shake until well blended.

Use a plastic drinking straw to hull strawberries with ease. Just push the straw through the end without a stem and the green, leafy top will pop right off!

Classic
Comfort
Foods

Delectable Chicken Divan

Marla Kinnersley
Highlands Ranch, CO

I came up with this delicious version of Chicken Divan and it has become a favorite for our family dinners. It's also perfect for taking to a family who needs a dinner. Everyone who tastes it wants my recipe!

5 chicken breasts
2 14-oz. pkgs. frozen broccoli
　flowerets
10-3/4 oz. can cream of chicken
　soup
1 c. mayonnaise
1 T. lemon juice

1 t. curry powder
8-oz. pkg. shredded Cheddar
　cheese
1/2 c. shredded Parmesan
　cheese
1 c. soft bread crumbs
1 T. butter, melted

In a large saucepan, cover chicken with water. Bring to a boil; reduce heat to low and simmer until chicken juices run clear. Drain; cool and cut chicken into one-inch cubes. Meanwhile, cook broccoli according to package directions; drain very well. Spray a 13"x9" baking pan lightly with non-stick vegetable spray. Add broccoli to pan; top with chicken and set aside. In a bowl, stir together soup, mayonnaise, lemon juice and curry powder. Spoon soup mixture over chicken; top with cheeses. In a small bowl, toss bread crumbs with butter; sprinkle over cheeses. Bake, uncovered, at 350 degrees for 30 to 40 minutes, until bubbly and golden. Makes 8 servings.

The number-one tip for fuss-free meals! Before you start cooking, read the recipe all the way through and make sure you have everything on hand that you'll need.

Updated Chicken Cordon Bleu

Ronda Hauss
Louisville, KY

My sister-in-law Tami shared this recipe with me when we were searching for healthier alternatives to add to our dinner menus. This one is a hit...it's fast and flavorful!

4 boneless, skinless chicken
  breasts
1 t. poultry seasoning
4 slices reduced-sodium
  deli ham

4 slices reduced-fat Jarlsberg
  or Swiss cheese
1/4 c. Dijon mustard
1/2 c. grated Parmesan cheese

Pound chicken breasts until flattened; season with poultry seasoning. Top each piece of chicken with one slice of ham and one slice of cheese. Roll up; fasten with one to 2 wooden toothpicks. Coat chicken rolls in mustard, then in grated cheese. Place chicken in a lightly greased, aluminum foil-lined shallow 8"x8" baking pan. Bake at 350 degrees for 30 to 35 minutes, until chicken juices run clear and cheese is melted. Makes 4 servings.

As a refreshing beverage, ice-cold tea can't be beat! Fill up a 2-quart pitcher with water and drop in 2 family-size tea bags. Refrigerate overnight. Discard tea bags and add sugar to taste; serve over ice.

Turkey with Penne Pasta

Linda Behling
Cecil, PA

This is a great-tasting, good-for-you recipe. I used to make it with ground beef, but changed it up by using ground turkey and a few other little tweaks. It's delicious...just add a tossed salad for a complete meal.

1 lb. whole-wheat penne
   or mezzi rigatoni pasta,
   uncooked
1 onion, chopped
2 T. olive oil
1 stalk celery, chopped
1 carrot, peeled and chopped

3 cloves garlic, minced
1 lb. lean ground turkey
28-oz. can crushed tomatoes
1/4 t. salt
1/4 t. pepper
1/4 c. fresh basil, chopped,
   or 1 T. dried basil

Cook pasta according to package directions; drain. Meanwhile, in a skillet over medium heat, sauté onion in oil until very soft, about 5 minutes. Add celery, carrot and garlic; sauté for another 5 minutes. Add turkey; increase heat to medium-high. Cook and stir until no longer pink. Add tomatoes with juice, salt and pepper. Cook until sauce thickens, stirring occasionally, about 20 minutes. Stir in basil just before serving. Serve turkey mixture ladled over cooked pasta. Makes 4 to 6 servings.

Good to know! Whole-wheat pasta has a much shorter shelf life than regular white pasta. For the best flavor and nutrition, use it within about 3 months of purchase.

Babcie's Cheesy Chicken Pot Pie
Barbara Cebula
Chicopee, MA

Every fall and winter I make this simple chicken pie. My family loves it. I got this recipe from my grandmother, who also handed it down to my mother.

3 c. cooked chicken, chopped
16-oz. pkg. frozen mixed
   vegetables, thawed and
   drained
8-oz. pkg. pasteurized process
   cheese, cubed

10-3/4 oz. can reduced-sodium
   cream of chicken soup
9-oz. tube refrigerated crescent
   rolls

In a lightly greased 13"x9" baking pan, combine chicken, vegetables, cheese and soup; mix gently. Unroll dough without separating rolls, place over chicken mixture to form a crust. Bake at 375 degrees for 20 to 25 minutes, until bubbly and crust is golden. Makes 8 servings.

Cut vents in your pot pie crust with a chicken-shaped
mini cookie cutter...so sweet.

All-In-One Pork Chop Dinner

Teresa Hallem
Manitoba, Canada

My mother used to fix this recipe for us when we were young. It's a quick way to make a delicious, veggie-packed meal all in one pan.

4 potatoes, peeled and quartered
2 to 3 carrots, peeled and cut
    into chunks
2 stems celery, cut into chunks
2 onions, quartered
1 to 2 cloves garlic, chopped
salt and pepper to taste
3/4 c. seasoned chicken coating
    mix
4 bone-in pork chops

Place vegetables in a lightly greased roasting pan or 13"x9" baking pan. Sprinkle with garlic, salt and pepper. Spread coating mix on a piece of wax paper; coat pork chops with coating mix. Place pork chops on top of vegetables. Cover and bake at 350 degrees for one hour, or until vegetables and pork chops are tender. Makes 4 servings.

For a tasty change, coat pork chops or chicken with grainy mustard and dredge them in finely ground pretzels before cooking.

Pork in Mustard Sauce

*Lynda Bolton
East Peoria, IL*

When our kids were home, I was all about quick & easy skillet meals, and this one was a favorite! I love it because I usually have most of the necessary ingredients on hand.

2 T. oil
4 to 6 bone-in or boneless pork
   chops
1 c. carrots, peeled and sliced
1 c. chicken broth
salt and pepper to taste

1 lb. sliced mushrooms
1/4 c. mustard
1/4 c. water
2 T. all-purpose flour
Optional: cooked rice or
   egg noodles

Heat oil in a large skillet over medium heat. Brown pork chops on both sides; drain. Meanwhile, place carrots in a microwave-safe bowl; add enough water to cover. Microwave for 2-1/2 to 3 minutes; drain and set aside. Pour chicken broth over pork chops in skillet; season with salt and pepper. Bring to a boil over medium-high heat. Add carrots and mushrooms to skillet; reduce heat to low. Cover and simmer until pork chops are tender, 30 to 40 minutes. Remove pork chops to a platter and cover to keep warm, reserving cooking juices in skillet. In a small bowl, combine mustard, water and flour; mix well. Pour mustard mixture into reserved juices in skillet. Cook and stir over medium heat for one to 2 minutes, until thickened. To serve, spoon thickened sauce over pork chops and cooked rice or noodles, if desired. Makes 4 to 6 servings.

Excess moisture can keep meat from browning well. For the most delicious results, pat it dry with a paper towel first.

Cheesy Ham & Cauliflower Bake
Molly Ebert
Columbus, IN

My guests gobble up this lighter version of scalloped potatoes!
The cauliflower makes for a nice change from potatoes.

2 10-oz. pkgs. frozen
  cauliflower, thawed and well
  drained
1-1/4 c. cooked ham, cubed
10-3/4 oz. can Cheddar cheese
  soup

1/4 c. milk
2/3 c. biscuit baking mix
2 T. butter, softened
2 T. shredded Cheddar cheese
1/2 t. nutmeg
paprika to taste

Arrange cauliflower in a lightly greased 11"x7" baking pan; top with
ham. In a bowl, whisk together soup and milk until smooth; pour over
ham. In a separate bowl, combine biscuit mix, butter, cheese and
nutmeg. Mix until crumbly and sprinkle over soup mixture. Sprinkle
with paprika. Bake, uncovered, at 400 degrees for 20 to 25 minutes,
until topping is golden. Makes 6 to 8 servings.

Often, casserole recipes call for precooked chicken, ham or
roast beef. For a handy recipe shortcut, stop at the deli counter
and order thick-sliced meat...it's ready to cube or chop as needed.

Pork Tenderloin Towers

Pearl Teiserskas
Brookfield, IL

I received this delicious recipe from a dear friend of mine back in 1951. She passed away in 2004, but each time I make this dish I still think about her.

6 pork tenderloin patties or
   pork cutlets
1 t. salt
1/4 t. pepper

6 thin slices onion
6 slices tomato
6 slices sharp Cheddar cheese
6 slices bacon, cut in half

Season patties with salt and pepper. Place in a lightly greased 13"x9" baking pan. Top each patty with a slice of onion, tomato and cheese. Criss-cross 2 half-slices of bacon on top of each patty; use a wooden toothpick to hold in place. Bake, covered, at 350 degrees for one hour. Uncover and bake for 15 minutes longer, or until pork is tender and bacon is crisp. Makes 6 servings.

Pour bacon drippings into a jar and store in the fridge. Add a spoonful or two when cooking hashbrown potatoes, green beans or pan gravy for wonderful down-home flavor.

Meatloaf-Stuffed Peppers

Janet Sharp
Milford, OH

My family loves these peppers stuffed with a meatloaf mixture and covered with tomato sauce. They're nice for lunch or dinner guests too. Serve with macaroni & cheese or steamed rice.

1 lb. ground beef or turkey
1/2 c. soft bread crumbs
1/4 c. catsup
3 T. onion, finely minced
1 egg, beaten
1/2 t. garlic powder
1 t. salt

1/4 t. pepper
4 to 6 green or red peppers,
   tops removed
15-1/2 oz. can crushed
   tomatoes, divided
1/4 c. grated Parmesan cheese

In a large bowl, combine beef or turkey, bread crumbs, catsup, onion, egg and seasonings. Mix gently with your hands just until combined. Loosely stuff each pepper; set aside. Thinly spread half of crushed tomatoes with juice in the bottom of a lightly greased 13"x9" baking pan. Place stuffed peppers in pan. Spoon remaining tomatoes over peppers; sprinkle evenly with Parmesan cheese. Cover with aluminum foil. Bake at 350 degrees for about one hour, until peppers are tender and meat mixture is no longer pink in the center. Makes 4 to 6 servings.

Stuffed green peppers will stand upright nicely when arranged in a tube cake pan before baking.

Steak Cantonese

Kim Hartless
Forest, VA

This is a recipe that my mom made often when we children were growing up. I still love it!

2 T. oil
1-1/2 lbs. beef round steak,
   thinly sliced into strips on
   the diagonal
2 tomatoes, coarsely chopped
2 green peppers, cut into strips
1/4 c. soy sauce

1/2 t. ginger
1/2 t. garlic salt
1/2 t. pepper
1 T. cornstarch
1/4 c. cold water
1 cube beef bouillon
cooked rice

Heat oil in a large skillet over high heat. Add beef strips and brown on all sides; drain. Reduce heat to medium-low; stir in tomatoes, green peppers, soy sauce and seasonings. Cover and simmer for 10 minutes. In a cup, blend cornstarch and water together. Stir cornstarch mixture into beef mixture; add bouillon cube. Cook and stir until mixture thickens and bouillon cube dissolves. Cover and simmer 10 minutes longer, or until beef is tender. Serve over cooked rice. Makes 4 servings.

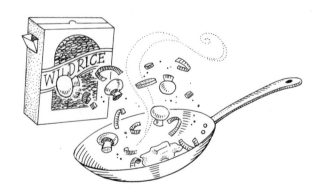

Turn a packaged wild rice mix into your own special blend in a jiffy. Sauté a cup of chopped mushrooms, onion and celery in butter until tender. Add the rice mix and prepare as the package directs.

Millie's Speedy Supper

Barbara Imler
Noblesville, IN

This is a recipe from my childhood that my working mother could put on the table quickly, so we had it often. It's still one of my favorite comfort foods. While it's simmering, make some mashed potatoes and a lettuce salad to go with it. A complete meal ready to serve in half an hour!

1 lb. ground beef chuck	3 onions, coarsely chopped
1/2 c. old-fashioned oats, uncooked	1-1/2 c. catsup
	1/3 c. vinegar
1 egg, beaten	1 t. sugar
1/2 t. garlic salt	1/2 t. salt
1/4 t. pepper	mashed potatoes

In a bowl, combine beef, oats, egg, garlic salt and pepper. Mix well with your hands. Form into golfball-size balls and flatten into patties. Add patties to a skillet over medium heat. Cook without turning, until very well browned; turn and cook other side. Remove patties to a plate. Drain skillet, reserving 2 tablespoons drippings. Add onions to reserved drippings; reduce heat to medium-low. Cook until onions start to soften but not brown, about 4 minutes. Stir in catsup, vinegar, sugar and salt; return patties to skillet. Simmer for 5 minutes. Serve patties and onion gravy from skillet with mashed potatoes. Makes 4 servings.

Keep browned ground beef on hand for easy meal prep. Just crumble several pounds of beef into a baking pan and bake at 350 degrees until browned through, stirring often. Drain well and pack recipe-size portions in freezer bags.

Comfort Foods

Cornbread Cowboy Casserole

Jenny Bishoff
Mountain Lake Park, MD

*I modified the original biscuit-topped Cowboy Casserole when
I couldn't find refrigerated biscuits my daughter Sophie
wasn't allergic to. We like this new version much better!*

1 lb. ground beef
16-oz. can baked beans
1/2 c. barbecue sauce

1/4 c. brown sugar, packed
8-1/2 oz. pkg. corn muffin mix
14-3/4 oz. can creamed corn

Brown beef in a Dutch oven or skillet over medium heat; drain. Stir in
baked beans, barbecue sauce and brown sugar; heat through. If using
a skillet, transfer mixture to a greased 2-quart casserole dish; set aside.
In a bowl, stir together dry cornbread mix and creamed corn; pour over
beef mixture. Bake, uncovered, at 400 degrees for 20 to 25 minutes,
until topping is cooked through. Serves 4 to 6.

Hamburger & Zucchini

Julie Bell
Fruit Heights, UT

*This is my favorite quick recipe for a zucchini main dish. It really
is a comfort food and so satisfying!*

1-1/2 lbs. ground beef
1 onion, chopped
1-1/2 lbs. zucchini, cubed
3/4 c. milk

10-3/4 oz. can cream of
    mushroom soup
8-oz. pkg. shredded Cheddar
    cheese

Brown beef in a skillet over medium heat; drain. Add onion and cook
until onion is glossy. In a buttered 3-quart casserole dish, layer
zucchini and beef mixture. Whisk together milk and soup; spoon over
top. Sprinkle with cheese. Bake, uncovered, at 350 degrees for about
30 minutes, until bubbly. Serves 4 to 5.

Humidity can cause salt to clump in the shaker. Add five or ten
grains of rice to your salt shaker to keep it free-flowing.

Zucchini Lasagna Rolls

Courtney Stultz
Columbus, KS

We love lasagna but wanted to try a lightened-up version. These Zucchini Lasagna Rolls are perfect...gluten-free, grain-free and loaded with veggies! Serve with a fresh spinach salad.

1 to 2 large zucchini, ends
   trimmed
1 c. ricotta cheese
4 roma tomatoes, diced
2 c. tomato sauce

1 T. tomato paste
1 t. Italian seasoning
salt and pepper to taste
Optional: 1 to 2 c. shredded
   Cheddar cheese

Use a mandoline slicer or a box grater to cut zucchini lengthwise into thin strips. Lay zucchini strips flat on a cutting board. Spread a layer of ricotta cheese over each strip; roll up tightly. Place rolls seam-side down in a greased 9"x9" baking pan. Any leftover ricotta cheese may be spooned over zucchini rolls. In a bowl, combine remaining ingredients; spoon over zucchini rolls. Season with a little salt and pepper; sprinkle with cheese, if desired. Bake, uncovered, at 325 degrees for 25 to 30 minutes. Makes 4 servings.

Potluck dinners are a wonderful way to share fellowship with family & friends. Why not make a standing date once a month to try new recipes as well as tried & true favorites?

Celebration Spaghetti

Vickie

Years ago, I clipped this recipe from a magazine ad and made it often. Recently I rediscovered it while going through my recipes. It's just as good as it was then...packed with fresh veggies and perfect for Meatless Monday meals.

16-oz. pkg. thin spaghetti,
   uncooked
1 T. olive oil
2 zucchini, diced
2 c. mushrooms, diced
1 c. black olives, sliced
1 green pepper, diced
28-oz. can diced tomatoes

2 6-oz. cans tomato paste
1/4 c. grated Parmesan cheese
1/2 t. Italian seasoning
1 t. salt
1/4 t. pepper
Garnish: additional grated
   Parmesan cheese

Cook spaghetti according to package directions; drain. Meanwhile, heat oil in a large skillet over medium heat. Sauté zucchini, mushrooms, olives and green pepper; drain. Stir in tomatoes with juice, tomato paste, Parmesan cheese and seasonings. Reduce heat to low. Simmer for 15 minutes, stirring occasionally. Serve sauce over cooked spaghetti, topped with Parmesan cheese. Makes 8 servings.

One of the very nicest things about life is the way
we must regularly stop whatever it is we are doing
and devote our attention to eating.
-Luciano Pavarotti

113

Guilt-Free Macaroni & Cheese

Wendy Perry
Midland, VA

In an effort to eat a more nutritious diet, I've discovered Greek yogurt is a fantastic substitute for sour cream and butter in sauces without losing the creamy goodness. We serve with a garden salad for a healthful, satisfying dinner.

1 c. whole-wheat macaroni,
   uncooked
1/3 c. plain non-fat Greek
   yogurt
1 t. garlic powder
1 t. onion powder
1 t. dry mustard

Optional: 1/4 t. cayenne pepper
1 c. shredded reduced-fat
   Cheddar cheese
salt and pepper to taste
1/4 c. whole-wheat panko bread
   crumbs
1/4 c. grated Parmesan cheese

Cook macaroni according to package directions, just until tender; drain and transfer to a bowl. In a cup, mix yogurt and seasonings. Spoon yogurt mixture over cooked macaroni. Stir in Cheddar cheese; season with salt and pepper. Transfer mixture to an 8"x8" baking pan sprayed with non-stick vegetable spray. Top with bread crumbs and Parmesan cheese. Bake, uncovered, at 425 degrees for 10 to 15 minutes, until heated through and golden on top. Makes 2 to 4 servings.

Find an old-fashioned chalkboard to announce "Today's Special."
It adds a whimsical diner feel hanging in the kitchen and
lets the whole family know what's for dinner.

Classic
Comfort Foods

Angel Hair Pasta & Veggies

Glorya Hendrickson
Hesperia, CA

This recipe came about when I decided to add veggies to some pasta and make it a filling, meatless meal. My family loves this dish and we don't even miss the meat!

3 T. olive oil, divided
1 zucchini, chopped
1 yellow squash, chopped
1 green pepper, chopped
1 onion, chopped
2 to 3 cloves garlic, minced

24-oz. jar marinara pasta sauce
16-oz. pkg. angel hair pasta, uncooked
Optional: grated Parmesan or Romano cheese

Heat 2 tablespoons oil in a large skillet or Dutch oven over medium heat. Sauté vegetables and garlic until crisp-tender; drain. Stir in pasta sauce. Reduce heat to low. Cover and simmer for about 30 minutes, stirring occasionally, until thickened. Meanwhile, cook pasta according to package directions; drain and toss with remaining oil. Serve vegetable mixture over cooked pasta. Top with grated cheese, if desired. Makes 6 servings.

There's no need to rinse pasta after cooking if it will be served immediately in a hot dish. Unrinsed pasta holds every drop of delicious sauce much better.

Baked Teriyaki Chicken

Teresa Verell
Roanoke, VA

This recipe is always requested for our New Year's Day supper...
but it's too tasty not to enjoy year 'round! Don't skip the
aluminum foil as it will save you a lot of clean-up time.

1 T. cornstarch	1/4 c. cider vinegar
1 T. cold water	1/4 t. ginger
1/2 c. low-sodium soy sauce	1/8 t. garlic powder, or to taste
1/4 c. sugar	1/8 t. pepper
1/4 c. light brown sugar, packed	12 chicken thighs, skin removed

In a small saucepan over low heat; combine all ingredients except
chicken. Simmer, stirring frequently, until sauce thickens and bubbles.
Meanwhile, line a 13"x9" baking pan with aluminum foil; spray lightly
with non-stick vegetable spray. Arrange chicken thighs in pan. Brush
chicken with sauce; turn pieces over and brush again. Bake,
uncovered, at 425 degrees for 30 minutes. Brush with sauce every
10 minutes during cooking. Turn chicken over; bake for another
30 minutes, continuing to brush with sauce, until chicken is no longer
pink and juices run clear. Makes 6 servings.

Chicken thighs are extra flavorful, juicy and easy on the budget,
but are usually sold with the bone in. To speed up cooking time,
use a sharp knife to make a deep cut on each side of the bone.

Comfort Foods

Fruity Dijon Chicken

Irene Robinson
Cincinnati, OH

A quick & easy stovetop recipe using pantry ingredients...great when you don't want to turn on the oven. Serve over cooked rice.

2/3 c. water
1/4 c. Dijon mustard
3 T. apricot or pineapple
   preserves

1 T. soy sauce
1 T. green onions, chopped
4 boneless, skinless chicken
   breasts

In a large skillet over medium-high heat, combine all ingredients except chicken. Stir well; add chicken and heat through. Reduce heat to low. Cover and simmer gently until chicken is tender and juices run clear, stirring occasionally, 20 to 30 minutes. Serves 4.

Herbed Chicken & Honey Butter

Ann Mathis
Biscoe, AR

Fast and easy, good on a weeknight when time is short. I often double the recipe, because my family loves it.

1 egg
3/4 c. seasoned dry bread
   crumbs
2 T. dried parsley
1 t. Italian seasoning

4 boneless, skinless chicken
   breasts
7 T. butter, softened and divided
1/4 c. honey

Place egg in a shallow bowl; beat lightly. In another shallow bowl, combine bread crumbs and seasonings. Dip chicken into egg; coat with crumb mixture. In a large skillet over medium heat, melt 3 tablespoons butter. Add chicken; cook for 4 to 5 minutes on each side, until golden and juices run clear. For Honey Butter, blend remaining butter and honey in a small bowl; serve with chicken. Makes 4 servings.

Always use tongs, not a fork, to turn chicken pieces in the pan...the savory juices won't run out.

Skillet Poppy Seed Chicken

Gail Blain Peterson
Stockton, NE

Mom used to make a similar recipe but it called for cream soup and crackers. This version calls for simple pantry items and is even better! My kids request this dish when comfort food is in order.

1 T. olive oil	2 T. butter
3 to 4 boneless, skinless chicken breasts	1/2 lb. sliced mushrooms
	3 T. all-purpose flour
salt and pepper to taste	1-1/2 c. chicken broth
1 shallot, minced	8-oz. container sour cream
1/2 c. dry white wine or chicken broth	2-oz. jar diced pimentos, drained

Heat oil in a large cast-iron skillet over medium-high heat. Season chicken with salt and pepper. Cook chicken on both sides until golden and juices run clear. Remove chicken to a plate; cover and set aside. To drippings in skillet, add shallot and wine or 1/2 cup broth. Cook until shallot is softened, scraping up browned bits in the bottom of skillet. Add butter and mushrooms; sauté until tender. Sprinkle flour into skillet; cook and stir until blended. Add broth; cook and stir until thickened. Stir in sour cream and pimentos. Slice chicken; return to skillet along with any juices from plate. Remove from heat. Sprinkle Topping over chicken; place skillet in oven. Bake, uncovered, at 350 degrees for 20 to 25 minutes, until heated through and topping is golden. Makes 6 servings.

Topping:

1/2 c. butter, melted	2 t. poppy seed
1-1/2 c. panko bread crumbs	

In a small bowl, combine all ingredients.

Store unwashed mushrooms in the refrigerator. The mushrooms will stay fresher longer if they're placed in a paper bag.

Chicken, Rice & Broccoli Casserole

Kathy Courington
Canton, GA

Every time I make this dish, I get compliments. It is simple and good. Once I took it to the hospital for friends and they loved it. The recipe is easily doubled in a 13"x9" baking pan for larger families or potlucks. Try it with leftover turkey too.

10-oz. pkg. frozen cut broccoli, thawed
1-1/2 c. hot cooked white or brown rice
1 c. cooked chicken breast, diced
1/2 onion, chopped
10-3/4 oz. can low-fat or low-sodium cream of chicken soup
1/4 c. fat-free milk
1/4 t. lemon pepper

In a large bowl, combine broccoli, rice, chicken and onion. Add soup, milk and lemon pepper; mix gently to combine. Spoon into an 8"x8" baking pan coated with non-stick butter-flavored vegetable spray. Bake, uncovered, at 350 degrees for 45 minutes, or until hot and bubbly. Cool pan on a wire rack for 5 minutes before serving. Makes 4 servings.

A quick homemade white sauce can replace "cream of" soup in recipes. Melt 2 tablespoons butter in a saucepan over low heat. Whisk in 2 tablespoons all-purpose flour until smooth, then add 2 cups milk. Cook and stir until thickened; add salt & pepper to taste. Shredded cheese, chopped cooked chicken or sautéed mushrooms can be added to the sauce too.

119

Country-Style Pork Chops

Shirley Howie
Foxboro, MA

This simple dish makes such a flavorful gravy...it's great served with mashed potatoes! I have been making this for many years now, and it is even a worthy dish for casual entertaining.

1 T. butter
6 pork loin chops, trimmed
10-1/2 oz. can beef broth
1/4 t. dried sage
1/4 t. dried thyme
1/4 t. salt

2 onions, sliced
2 c. carrots, peeled and sliced
    on the diagonal
1 c. celery, sliced on the diagonal
1/4 c. cornstarch
1-1/4 c. milk

Melt butter in a large skillet over medium heat. Brown pork chops on both sides. Stir together broth and seasonings in a bowl; pour over pork chops. Arrange vegetables over pork chops. Reduce heat to low. Cover and simmer for 50 minutes, or until tender. Remove pork chops to a plate, reserving drippings in skillet; keep warm. Combine cornstarch and milk in a cup; mix well and stir into mixture in pan. Cook and stir until sauce thickens; spoon over pork chops. Serves 6.

If mashed potatoes are on the dinner menu, whip in a teaspoon or so of baking powder and they'll be extra light and fluffy.

Saucy Pork, Peppers & Pasta

Tori Willis
Champaign, IL

A wonderful one-skillet meal that's out of the ordinary!
Sometimes I'll jazz it up with curly cavatappi pasta.

12-oz. pkg. penne pasta,
  uncooked
2 T. olive oil, divided
1 green pepper, cut into strips
1 red pepper, cut into strips
1 onion, cut into wedges
4 center-cut pork chops

salt and pepper to taste
1/2 c. all-purpose flour
26-oz. jar tomato & roasted
  garlic pasta sauce
1/2 c. white wine or chicken
  broth
1/2 t. dried thyme

Cook pasta according to package directions; drain. Meanwhile, heat one tablespoon oil in a large skillet over medium-high heat. Cook peppers and onion until crisp-tender. Remove vegetables to a bowl and set aside. Season pork chops lightly with salt and pepper; coat with flour. Add remaining oil to skillet; brown pork chops on both sides. Reduce heat to low; stir in pasta sauce, wine or broth and thyme. Cover and simmer for 30 minutes, stirring occasionally, or until pork chops are tender. Remove pork chops to a plate. Stir vegetable mixture into sauce mixture and heat through. Serve pork chops and sauce over cooked pasta. Makes 4 servings.

Keep a large shaker of seasoned flour close at hand for sprinkling on pork chops and chicken before frying. A good mix is one cup flour, 1/4 cup seasoned salt and one tablespoon pepper.

Mom's Cheesy Scalloped Potatoes & Ham

Lori Niver
Webster, NY

This is my most-requested recipe, my family's ultimate comfort food. I use non-stick aluminum foil to cover the dish while baking. I don't want to waste one single drop of sauce or one potato!

8 T. butter, divided
6 T. all-purpose flour
1 t. salt
1/2 t. pepper
4 c. milk
2 c. shredded sharp Cheddar
  cheese

8 potatoes, peeled and thinly
  sliced
1 onion, thinly sliced
2 to 2-1/2 lbs. cooked ham,
  sliced 1/4-inch thick

Melt 6 tablespoons butter in a medium saucepan over low heat. Blend in flour, salt and pepper. Cook over low heat, stirring constantly, until mixture is smooth and bubbly. Stir in milk until boiling, stirring constantly. Boil and stir for one minute. Remove from heat; stir in cheese until melted. Grease a 13"x9" baking pan with one tablespoon butter. Layer 1/3 of potatoes in pan; top with half of the onion, half of the ham and 1/3 of the cheese sauce. Repeat layers twice, ending with remaining potatoes and sauce. Dot with remaining butter. Cover with non-stick aluminum foil. Bake at 350 degrees for 30 minutes. Remove foil and cook until potatoes are tender, 60 to 70 minutes longer. Let stand 5 to 10 minutes before serving. Makes 6 servings.

Get a head start on dinner by peeling and cutting up potatoes the night before. They won't turn dark if you cover them with water before refrigerating them.

122

Comfort Foods

Ham, Bacon, Cabbage & Noodle Dish

Kathleen Whitsett
Greenwood, IN

Comfort in a skillet! This is a variation on a recipe from my grandmother and my mother, who are both wonderful cooks. I love the tastes and textures of this recipe and the shredded carrots give it a pop of color. Serve family-style in a large bowl with slices of buttered warm French bread.

16 to 24-oz. pkg. wide egg
    noodles, uncooked
8 slices bacon, diced
2 T. butter , sliced
1 T. olive oil
1 onion, chopped

1 c. carrot, peeled and shredded
1 clove garlic, minced
1 head cabbage, shredded
2 c. cooked ham, diced
salt and pepper to taste

Cook egg noodles according to package directions; drain. Meanwhile, in a large skillet over medium heat, cook bacon until crisp. Remove bacon to a paper towel, reserving one tablespoon drippings in skillet. Add butter and olive oil to drippings; stir. Add onion; cook until onion begins to soften, stirring often. Add carrot; cook until carrot begins to soften, stirring often. Add cabbage; cook until cabbage begins to soften, stirring often. Add garlic; cook and stir for one minute. Add ham and bacon; reduce heat to low. Simmer for a few minutes, until heated through. Add cooked noodles and stir gently. Season with salt and pepper. Makes 4 to 6 servings.

Longing for Mom's old-fashioned homemade egg noodles? Try frozen egg noodles from your grocer's frozen food section. Thicker and heartier than dried noodles, these homestyle noodles cook up quickly in all your favorite recipes.

Sunday Meatball Skillet

Eugenia Taylor
Stroudsburg, PA

My mother-in-law Ann shared this hearty recipe with me when I first got married. It's a mainstay in our monthly rotation menu.

8-oz. pkg. medium egg noodles, uncooked
3/4 lb. ground beef
1 c. onion, grated
1/2 c. Italian-flavored dry bread crumbs
1 egg, beaten

1/4 c. catsup
1/4 t. pepper
2 c. beef broth
1/4 c. all-purpose flour
1/2 c. sour cream
Garnish: chopped fresh parsley

Cook egg noodles according to package directions; drain. Meanwhile, in a bowl, combine beef, onion, bread crumbs, egg, catsup and pepper. Mix well with your hands; form into one-inch meatballs. Spray a large skillet with non-stick vegetable spray. Cook meatballs over medium heat, turning occasionally, until browned, about 10 minutes. Remove meatballs and drain on paper towels, reserving drippings in skillet. In a bowl, whisk together broth and flour; add to skillet. Cook and stir over medium heat until mixture thickens, about 5 minutes. Stir in sour cream. Add meatballs and cooked noodles; toss to coat. Cook and stir until heated through, about 5 minutes. Garnish with parsley.

Making lots of mini meatballs? Grab a melon baller and start scooping...you'll be done in record time!

Meatball Sub Casserole

Audra Vanhorn-Sorey
Columbia, NC

A fun twist on an all-American favorite!

8-oz. pkg. cream cheese,
  softened
1 loaf Italian bread, sliced 1-inch
  thick
2 c. shredded mozzarella cheese,
  divided

28-oz. jar pasta sauce
1/4 c. water
16-oz. pkg. frozen meatballs,
  thawed
1 t. Italian seasoning
1/4 t. pepper

Spread cream cheese over one side of bread slices. Arrange cheese-side up in the bottom of a lightly greased 13"x9" baking pan. Top bread evenly with one cup mozzarella cheese. In a bowl, mix pasta sauce with water; spread evenly over cheese. Arrange meatballs on top. Sprinkle with seasonings and remaining cheese. Bake, uncovered, at 350 degrees for 25 to 30 minutes, until heated through and cheese is melted. Makes 6 servings.

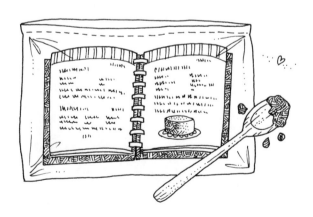

To keep your cookbook splatter-free and open to
the page you're using, just slide it inside a
large plastic zipping bag.

Turkey-Sausage Meatloaf

Pearl Teiserskas
Brookfield, IL

My family & friends always request this meatloaf when I bring it to our church socials. The recipe was handed down from my grandmother, who was a wonderful cook. It is not only easy to make, but delicious and filled with good-for-you ingredients.

1-1/2 lbs. ground turkey	1 clove garlic, chopped
1 lb. ground pork sausage	1 t. dried thyme
10-oz. pkg. frozen spinach,	1 t. dried marjoram
thawed and squeezed dry	1 t. salt
1 onion, chopped	3/4 t. pepper
2 to 3 carrots, peeled and	1/2 c. dry bread crumbs
chopped	2 eggs, beaten

In a large bowl, combine all ingredients except bread crumbs and eggs; mix well. Add bread crumbs and eggs; mix thoroughly. Pack mixture loosely into a lightly greased 9"x5" loaf pan, rounding top slightly. Bake at 350 degrees for about one hour and 15 minutes, until a meat thermometer reads 160 degrees when inserted in center of meatloaf. Drain any fat; turn meatloaf onto a cutting board. Slice into thick slices. Serve hot or cold. Makes 8 servings.

Sneak some veggies into your next meatloaf for added nutrition. Sauté finely chopped carrot, celery and onion until tender. Add to the meat mixture and prepare as usual... the kids probably won't notice!

Gluten-Free Meatloaf Pie

Hope Davenport
Portland, TX

Everybody enjoys this meatloaf pie! We created this gluten-free version when our youngest son was diagnosed with celiac disease.

5-oz. can evaporated milk
1/2 c. gluten-free dry bread
  crumbs
1/2 t. garlic salt
1 lb. lean ground beef
1/3 c. gluten-free pasta sauce or
  catsup

1 c. shredded Cheddar cheese
1/2 c. shredded mozzarella
  cheese
1 to 2 T. grated Parmesan
  cheese

Combine evaporated milk, bread crumbs and garlic salt in a large bowl. Add beef and mix gently. Press into a lightly greased 9" pie plate to form a shell. Bake, uncovered, at 350 degrees for 25 minutes, or until beef is no longer pink. Spread with pasta sauce or catsup; top with cheeses. Bake an additional 5 minutes, or until cheese is melted. Let stand for several minutes; cut into wedges. Makes 4 servings.

It's simple to substitute fresh baby spinach in recipes that call for frozen chopped spinach. Simply add 10 ounces of fresh spinach and 2 tablespoons water to a saucepan. Cook over medium-low heat for 3 minutes. Stir gently until wilted, then rinse in cold water, drain and squeeze dry.

Spinach Linguine with Sun-Dried Tomatoes

Eleanor Dionne
Beverly, MA

This is a quick meatless meal. Kids like the green noodles!

16-oz. pkg. spinach linguine, uncooked
1 bunch green onions, chopped
1 T. olive oil
6 plum tomatoes, diced
8 oil-packed sun-dried tomatoes, drained and coarsely chopped

1/3 t. dried oregano
2 T. fresh basil, thinly sliced
2 T. fresh parsley, chopped
2 to 3 cloves garlic
salt and pepper to taste
Garnish: 4-oz. pkg. crumbled goat cheese or feta cheese

Cook pasta according to package directions; drain. Meanwhile, in a large skillet over medium heat, sauté green onions in oil until tender; drain. Stir in remaining ingredients except cheese. Simmer over low heat for 3 minutes. Season with salt and pepper. Serve sauce over cooked pasta; top with cheese, if desired. Serves 4.

Easy Garlic Spaghetti

Lisa Langston
Conroe, TX

I found this easy dish in an old cookbook. It is quite tasty and it is meatless, which I really like.

2 t. olive oil
4 cloves garlic, minced
2 T. butter, sliced
3 c. chicken or vegetable broth
1/4 t. salt

1/2 t. pepper
8-oz. pkg. spaghetti, uncooked
1 c. grated Parmesan cheese
3/4 c. whipping cream
1-1/2 T. dried parsley

In a large saucepan, heat olive over medium heat. Add garlic; cook and stir for one to 2 minutes. Stir in butter, broth, salt and pepper; bring to a boil. Add pasta; cook for about 10 minutes, until tender. Add a little more broth if spaghetti starts to stick. Drain; add Parmesan cheese, cream and parsley. Toss to mix well. Serves 6.

Spaghetti-Style Squash Casserole

Elizabeth Smithson
Cunningham, KY

When my kids were home, I would serve this recipe to get them to eat veggies they didn't think they liked! This was a favorite.

1 yellow squash, peeled
  and cubed
1 zucchini, peeled and cubed
1 lb. ground beef chuck
1 green pepper, diced
1/2 c. onion, chopped
1 clove garlic, minced

14-1/2 oz. can Italian-seasoned
  diced tomatoes
1/2 t. dried oregano, or more
  to taste
1/2 t. dried basil
salt and pepper to taste
2 c. shredded Cheddar cheese

Add squash and zucchini to a food processor; process until shredded. Squeeze out any liquid with paper towels. In a large skillet over medium heat, brown beef with green pepper, onion and garlic; drain. Add squash mixture, tomatoes with juice and seasonings; heat to boiling, stirring often. Transfer mixture to a 2-quart casserole dish sprayed with non-stick vegetable spray. Top with cheese. Bake, uncovered, at 350 degrees for 30 to 35 minutes, until bubbly and cheese is melted. Makes 6 to 8 servings.

A crunchy topping makes any casserole even tastier. Savory cracker crumbs, crushed tortilla chips or toasted, buttered bread crumbs are all delicious...just sprinkle on before baking. Leave the casserole uncovered so the topping will bake up crisp and golden.

Penne With Tomato Cream Sauce

Donna Smith
Wilmington, DE

This is a very rich-tasting recipe that has only one gram of fat and 225 calories, but tastes like much much more. It is the basic comfort pasta without the guilt...meatless, but you won't miss the meat. It's made on the stovetop, not baked, so it's quick to fix.

16-oz. pkg. penne pasta, uncooked
1 red pepper, cut into strips
1 yellow pepper, cut into strips
1 onion, sliced thinly
2 cloves garlic, minced
1 T. olive oil
14-1/2 oz. can diced tomatoes, plain or with green chiles

1 t. sugar
1 t. dried basil
1/4 t. salt
1/4 t. pepper
2 t. all-purpose flour
1/2 c. fat-free evaporated milk
Garnish: additional dried basil

Cook pasta according to package directions; drain. Meanwhile, in a skillet over medium heat, sauté peppers, onion and garlic in oil until tender. Add tomatoes with juice, sugar and seasonings; bring to a boil. Whisk together flour and evaporated milk in a bowl; add to tomato mixture. Cover and cook for 5 minutes; stir in cooked pasta. Add a little more milk, if too thick. Serve topped with a sprinkle of basil. Makes 6 servings.

Try this refreshing salad! Peel and thinly slice 3 cucumbers and one small red onion. Toss with 2 tablespoons chopped fresh dill and one tablespoon each lemon juice, vegetable oil and sugar. Season with 3/4 teaspoon salt and refrigerate, covered, for 2 hours before serving.

Comfort Foods

Easy Cheesy Manicotti

Elissa Ducar
Denton, TX

What I love about this recipe is the fact that you do not have to cook the pasta shells first. It's a good dish for Meatless Monday, if you are looking for new ideas.

24-oz. jar marinara pasta sauce
15-oz. container low-fat or
    fat-free ricotta cheese
1/4 c. shredded Pecorino
    Romano cheese
2 c. shredded reduced-fat
    mozzarella cheese, divided
1/2 c. egg substitute

1 t. dried parsley
1/2 t. dried basil
1/2 t. dried oregano
1/8 t. salt
1/4 t. pepper
14 manicotti pasta shells,
    uncooked
1 c. water

Spray a 13"x9" baking pan with non-stick vegetable spray. Spread half of pasta sauce evenly in bottom of pan; set aside. In a bowl, combine ricotta cheese, Pecorino Romano cheese, 1-1/2 cups shredded mozzarella cheese and egg substitute; stir until blended. Add seasonings; stir well and set aside. Stuff each uncooked manicotti shell with 3 tablespoons cheese mixture. Arrange stuffed shells in a single layer over sauce in pan. Spoon remaining sauce over shells; add water to pan. Sprinkle with remaining mozzarella cheese. Cover tightly with aluminum foil. Bake at 375 degrees for one hour, or until shells are tender. Let stand 10 minutes before serving. Makes 6 to 8 servings.

No-mess stuffed pasta shells! Spoon cheese filling into a plastic zipping bag. Clip off a corner of the bag and squeeze the filling into shells, then toss away the bag.

Quick-Fix Chicken Spaghetti

Beckie Apple
Grannis, AR

*I am always experimenting with dishes to prepare in the microwave.
My husband proclaimed this one a keeper. It's ready in less than
30 minutes and great served with a tossed salad.*

6 c. hot water
1 T. margarine
6-1/2 oz. can sliced mushrooms
1/4 c. onion, chopped
2 T. green pepper, diced
1/4 t. salt
12-oz. pkg. spaghetti, uncooked
   and broken in half

15-oz. jar 3-cheese Alfredo
   sauce
10-oz. can chicken breast,
   broken up
2 T. grated Parmesan cheese
1/8 t. pepper
Optional: additional grated
   Parmesan cheese

In a microwave-safe 2-quart bowl, combine hot water, margarine,
mushrooms with liquid, onion, green pepper and salt. Cover bowl
loosely with vented plastic wrap or a paper plate; microwave on high
for 8 minutes. Add spaghetti to bowl; stir slightly to break apart. Cover
loosely again; microwave for 5 minutes. Stir spaghetti mixture again;
cover and cook for another 4 to 6 minutes. Drain; add Alfredo sauce,
chicken with liquid, Parmesan cheese and pepper. Mix well and
transfer to a microwave-safe serving dish. Microwave, uncovered,
for another 3 minutes. At serving time, sprinkle with additional cheese,
if desired. Makes 6 servings.

Even a simple family supper can be memorable when it's
thoughtfully served. Use the good china, set out cloth napkins
and a vase of fresh flowers...after all, who's more special
than your family?

Chicken Bacon-Ranch Bake

Nicole Manley
Jacksonville, FL

I started dieting but love comfort foods, so I set out to create that feeling. This is one of the recipes I came up with that my whole family loves. Each portion is under 400 calories!

12-oz. pkg. frozen cauliflower
1/2 lb. boneless, skinless
   chicken breast, cooked
   and cubed
1 bunch green onions, chopped
2 T. light ranch salad dressing

1-1/2 c. shredded Colby-Jack
   cheese, divided
salt and pepper to taste
2 slices bacon, crisply cooked
   and crumbled

Cook cauliflower according to package directions; drain very well. In a bowl, combine cauliflower, chicken, green onions, salad dressing, 1-1/4 cups cheese, salt and pepper. Mix well; spoon into an 8"x8" baking pan sprayed with non-stick vegetable spray. Sprinkle bacon and remaining cheese on top. Cover and bake at 350 degrees for 30 minutes, or until heated through and cheese is melted. Makes 4 servings.

Turn refrigerated dinner rolls into a pull-apart treat at dinnertime. Cut rolls into 4 wedges and place them in a plastic zipping bag with grated Parmesan cheese and some zesty seasonings. Shake 'em up, pile into a greased casserole dish and bake as usual.

Southern-Style Smothered Chicken

Helen Adams
Enchanted Oaks, TX

I remember enjoying this dish at family gatherings as a child. The recipe has been handed down through the years and is a family favorite to this day.

3-1/2 lb. fryer chicken, cut up
2 t. salt, divided
1-1/2 c. all-purpose flour
1 t. paprika
1 t. dried thyme
1 t. pepper
1/2 t. garlic salt

1/2 t. poultry seasoning
3/4 c. oil
2 yellow onions, sliced
4 to 6 c. water
cooked rice
Garnish: fresh thyme

Sprinkle chicken with one teaspoon salt; set aside. In a shallow dish, combine flour, remaining salt and seasonings. Dredge chicken in flour mixture, coating well; shake off any excess. Reserve 3/4 cup remaining flour mixture. Heat oil in a Dutch oven over medium-high heat. Add chicken and cook until chicken is golden on all sides; drain on a paper towel. Drain and reserve oil from pan. Add onions and one tablespoon reserved oil; sauté for about 2 minutes. Remove onions to a dish to drain. Return 5 tablespoons reserved oil to pan. Stir in reserved flour mixture, a little at a time, until well blended. Cook and stir over medium heat until very thick. Blend in water, one cup at a time, to desired gravy consistency. Return chicken to pan; turn to make sure each piece is covered with gravy. Top with onions. Cover and bake at 350 degrees for one hour, stirring after 30 minutes, until chicken is very tender. Add more water if gravy is too thick. Serve chicken and gravy with cooked rice, garnished with thyme. Serves 6.

Comfort Foods

Chicken Eugene

Betty Kozlowski
Newnan, GA

*My oldest sister Priscilla shared this recipe with me many years ago
and it became an instant favorite with us! It's a great recipe for
company because the prep is very easy, yet it's delicious.*

8 chicken thighs and drumsticks
paprika and pepper to taste
8 thin slices deli turkey ham
8 thin slices Swiss cheese
10-3/4 oz. can cream of
   mushroom soup

8-oz. container sour cream
1/2 c. sherry or chicken broth
1/4 lb. sliced mushrooms, or
   4-oz. can sliced mushrooms,
   drained
cooked rice or egg noodles

Season chicken with paprika and pepper; set aside. Arrange ham
slices to cover the bottom of a greased 13"x9" baking pan; repeat with
cheese slices. Arrange chicken on top. In a bowl, whisk together soup,
sour cream and sherry or broth. Stir in mushrooms; spoon over
chicken. Cover and bake at 350 degrees for one to 1-1/2 hours, until
bubbly and chicken juices run clear. Serve over cooked rice or noodles.
Makes 8 servings.

For an extra taste of nostalgia, serve creamy chicken dishes
spooned over old-fashioned toast points. Trim the crusts from
thinly sliced bread, cut into triangles and bake at 425 degrees
until golden, 2 to 3 minutes per side.

Tanya's Pork Parmesan

Tanya Schroeder
Cincinnati, OH

Chicken Parmesan is one of my husband's favorite meals, and my whole family can eat a lot of pasta! I thought I'd change things up and try making the recipe with pork instead of chicken.

6 boneless pork loin chops
salt and pepper to taste
3/4 c. all-purpose flour
4-oz. container egg substitute
1/2 c. dry bread crumbs
1/2 c. panko bread crumbs
1/4 c. grated Parmesan cheese
3 T. olive oil, divided
1 c. shredded mozzarella cheese
16-oz. pkg. angel hair pasta, uncooked

Season pork chops with salt and pepper; set aside. Place flour and egg in two separate shallow bowls. Combine bread crumbs and Parmesan cheese in a third shallow bowl. Dip pork chops into flour, then egg, then bread crumb mixture. Heat oil in a large skillet over medium-high heat. Brown pork chops on both sides, about 5 to 7 minutes; drain. Arrange pork chops in a 3-quart casserole dish coated with non-stick vegetable spray. Ladle one cup Tomato Sauce over pork chops. Sprinkle pork chops with shredded cheese. Bake at 400 degrees for 15 minutes, or until cheese has melted. Cook pasta according to package directions; drain. Serve pork chops with remaining Tomato Sauce sauce over cooked pasta. Serves 6.

Tomato Sauce:

1 T. olive oil
2 cloves garlic, minced
28-oz. can crushed tomatoes
14-1/2 oz. can petite diced
   tomatoes
8-oz. can tomato sauce
2 t. sugar
1 t. Italian seasoning
1/4 t. red pepper flakes
1/2 t. salt

Heat oil in a small saucepan over medium heat. Add garlic; cook for one minute. Add crushed tomatoes with juice, diced tomatoes with juice and remaining ingredients. Cook until mixture begins to simmer. Reduce heat to low; cover until ready to use.

Pork & Brown Rice Dish

Gerri Roth
Flushing, MI

This recipe of my mother's is very satisfying on a cool evening.

2 T. butter
1 lb. boneless pork loin,
   cut into 1-inch cubes
1 c. onion, finely chopped
1 c. celery, finely chopped
10-3/4 oz. can cream of
   mushroom soup

14-oz. can chicken broth
1-1/2 c. water
1/2 c. long-cooking brown rice,
   uncooked
1/4 c. soy sauce

Melt butter in a skillet over medium heat. Add pork cubes and brown on all sides. Add onion and celery; cook and stir for 3 to 5 minutes. Transfer mixture to a greased 3-quart casserole dish; set aside. Combine remaining ingredients in a bowl; stir well and spoon over pork mixture. Stir gently. Cover and bake at 375 degrees for one to 1-1/2 hours, until pork and rice are tender. Makes 4 to 6 servings.

Garden-fresh vegetables are delicious prepared simply... steamed and topped with pats of lemon butter. Simply blend 2 tablespoons softened butter with the zest of one lemon.

137

Ham & Potato Gratin

Debbie Benzi
Binghamton, NY

My family is always happy when I make this dish. The sauce is rich and the cheese is gooey. It's the ultimate comfort food!

2-1/2 lbs. potatoes, peeled and
   sliced 1/8-inch thick
1-1/2 c. whipping cream
1 c. whole milk

1-1/2 t. salt
pepper to taste
1 lb. cooked ham, diced
2 c. shredded Cheddar cheese

Place potato slices in a bowl; set aside. Combine cream, milk and salt in a microwave-safe dish. Microwave for 2 minutes, or until warm; season with pepper. Pour warm cream mixture over potatoes; mix well. Add ham. Spoon into a greased 12"x9" baking pan. Sprinkle with cheese. Bake, uncovered, at 350 degrees for one hour, or until potatoes are fork-tender. Makes 6 servings.

Let the kids lend a hand in the kitchen. Preschoolers can wash veggies, fold napkins and set the table. Older children can measure, shred, chop, stir and maybe even help with meal planning and grocery shopping. Memories in the making...not to mention good habits!

Classic
Comfort Foods

Swiss Cheese Ziti Casserole

Diane Cohen
Breinigsville, PA

My mom gave me this recipe. It is quick, delicious and full of flavors my family loves. I make it often.

16-oz. pkg. ziti pasta, uncooked
   and divided
10-3/4 oz. can cream of celery
   soup

8-oz. container sour cream
1 c. shredded Swiss cheese
2 c. cooked ham, cubed

Cook half of pasta according to package directions; reserve remaining pasta for another recipe. Drain pasta; return to cooking pot. Add remaining ingredients; mix well. Transfer mixture to a greased 2-quart casserole dish. Bake, uncovered, at 350 degrees for 35 to 45 minutes, until bubbly and cheese is melted. Serves 4.

Ham & Broccoli Bake

Beth Bundy
Long Prairie, MN

My mom found this recipe in an old church cookbook... it's become a favorite of mine.

10-oz. loaf French bread, cubed
3/4 c. butter, melted
2 c. shredded Cheddar cheese,
   divided
10-oz. pkg. frozen chopped
   broccoli, thawed and divided

2 c. cooked ham, cubed
5 eggs
2 c. milk
1/4 t. pepper

In a bowl, toss bread cubes with melted butter. Place half of bread cubes in a lightly greased 13"x9" baking pan. Top with half the cheese, half the broccoli and all the ham. Top with remaining cheese, broccoli and bread cubes. In a separate bowl, whisk together eggs, milk and pepper; pour over top. Cover and refrigerate for one hour. Uncover; bake at 350 degrees for 40 to 45 minutes. Makes 8 to 10 servings.

Chicken & Dumplings

Tina Goodpasture
Meadowview, VA

In my book, southern chicken & dumplings can't be beat as the all-time best comfort food. My family loves chicken & dumplings and the more dumplings the better we like it! It brings back memories of my granny, who used to raise chickens on the farm.

10-3/4 oz. can cream of
  chicken soup
2 10-1/2 oz. cans chicken broth
4 c. water

4 c. cooked chicken or turkey,
  chopped
1 c. celery, chopped
salt and pepper to taste

Combine all ingredients except salt and pepper in a soup pot; bring to a boil over medium-high heat. Cover and simmer while preparing dough for Dumplings. Uncover pot. Add dumpling squares, several at a time, to the boiling broth. Cover again each time for about 30 seconds, until all the dumplings have been added. Reduce heat to low; simmer for about 20 minutes. Season with salt and pepper. Serves 6 to 8.

Dumplings:

2 c. self-rising flour
1/4 c. shortening

3/4 c. boiling water

Add flour to a large bowl. Cut in shortening with a pastry blender or fork. Add boiling water, a little at a time, until dough forms and can be shaped into a ball. On a floured surface, roll out dough, 1/8-inch thick. With a pizza cutter or a knife, cut dough into strips one-inch wide. Cut again to form one-inch squares.

Easy Chicken, Potatoes & Green Beans

Judy Beal
Dover, OH

*One of my favorite go-to recipes...scrumptious and
so easy to put together.*

3 boneless, skinless chicken
   breasts, cut in half
2 16-oz. cans green beans,
   drained
6 to 8 redskin potatoes,
   quartered

1-oz. pkg. zesty Italian salad
   dressing mix
1/2 c. butter, melted

In a lightly greased 13"x9" baking pan, arrange chicken pieces down center of pan. To one side of pan, add green beans. To the other side, add potatoes. Sprinkle salad dressing mix on top; drizzle melted butter over all. Cover with aluminum foil. Bake at 350 degrees for one hour, or until chicken juices run clear and potatoes are tender. Makes 6 servings.

If Grandma never wrote down her recipes, you can still make a scrapbook of family food memories. Ask for descriptions of favorite dishes...how they smelled, tasted and looked when they were served. Collect them in a scrapbook and add special photos of family meals. Who knows, maybe someone who looks at your scrapbook will have the recipes you miss!

Nanny's Hot Chicken Salad

Julie Hutson
Callahan, FL

My grandmother was the epitome of a southern hostess. Every person who ever walked through her door was offered a slice of pound cake or a homemade cookie. And she loved a party! Whenever someone mentioned they were planning a get-together, she would ask what she could bring. This is one of my all-time favorite recipes from her library.

3 boneless, skinless chicken
    breasts, cooked and cubed
2 c. cooked rice
2 c. shredded sharp Cheddar
    cheese
1 c. celery, chopped
1 c. mayonnaise

1/4 c. sour cream
1 T. lemon juice
1/2 t. salt
1/2 t. pepper
1/2 sleeve round buttery
    crackers, crushed
2 T. butter, melted

In a large bowl, mix together all ingredients except crackers and butter. Spoon into a 3-quart casserole dish coated with non-stick vegetable spray. Sprinkle crackers over top; drizzle melted butter over crackers. Bake at 350 degrees for 30 minutes, until bubbly and golden on top. Makes 8 to 10 servings.

Throw an apron party! Invite your best girlfriends to tie on their frilliest vintage aprons and join you in the kitchen to whip up a favorite dish together. It's a fun way to catch up with everyone while enjoying some yummy food.

Hawaiian Chicken

Mary Eichel
Carrollton, OH

*My mom used to make this simple dish when I was a little girl.
I still just love it with a fresh tossed salad.*

2 lbs. chicken breasts or thighs
salt and pepper to taste
1/3 c. steak sauce
2 T. honey

8-1/4 oz. can sliced pineapple,
    drained and 2 T. juice
    reserved

Place chicken in a greased 12"x7" baking pan; season with salt and
pepper. Bake, uncovered, at 400 degrees for 30 minutes, turning once.
Meanwhile, combine steak sauce, honey and reserved pineapple juice
in a small bowl; spoon over chicken. Bake, uncovered, an additional
25 minutes, basting occasionally. Arrange pineapple slices over
chicken; bake 10 minutes longer. Makes 4 to 6 servings.

Mom's Lemonade Chicken
JoAlice Patterson-Welton
Lawrenceville, GA

*My family always loved this chicken when Mom prepared it.
It's so light and juicy! Wonderful served with rice.*

6 boneless, skinless chicken
    breasts
1/3 c. soy sauce

6-oz. can frozen lemonade
    concentrate, thawed
1 t. garlic powder

Place chicken in a 13"x9" baking pan sprayed with non-stick vegetable
spray. Combine remaining ingredients in a bowl; spoon over chicken.
Cover and bake at 350 degrees for 45 minutes. Uncover; spoon pan
juices over chicken and cook for an additional 10 minutes. Makes
6 servings.

Keep sour cream fresh longer...store the container
upside-down in the fridge.

Lightened-Up Salisbury Steaks

Marsha Baker
Pioneer, OH

This dish is so full of flavor, no one will ever know they're eating a lightened-up recipe. It's ready in less than 30 minutes. Serve with mashed potatoes and a veggie for a very satisfying meal.

1/4 c. egg whites, beaten
1 onion, finely chopped
1/2 c. saltine crackers, crushed
1/2 t. pepper
1 lb. lean ground beef

Optional: 2 t. canola oil
2 c. water
1-oz. pkg. reduced-sodium
  onion soup mix
2 T. all-purpose flour

In a large bowl, combine egg whites, onion, crackers and pepper. Crumble beef over mixture and mix well. Shape into 5 patties. Heat a large non-stick skillet over medium heat, adding oil if desired. Cook patties for 3 minutes on each side, or until lightly browned. Remove patties to a plate and keep warm; drain drippings. Combine water, soup mix and flour in same skillet; mix well. Bring to a boil, stirring constantly. Return patties to skillet. Reduce heat; cover and simmer for 5 to 7 minutes, until beef is no longer pink. Makes 5 servings.

Blue Willow is a classic vintage china pattern, so soothing to the eye...why not start a collection of pieces from tag sales and thrift shops? Your mix & match finds are sure to blend together on the dinner table.

Comfort Foods

Mother's Goulash

Geraldine Weedman
Caldwell, ID

This recipe has been in my mother's family for a long time. It is easy to make and it always tastes just as good when it is reheated. It has been revised several times...everyone adds or changes something in it. I use fresh tomatoes and green onions whenever I can get them. I have even revised it to use ground turkey and whole-wheat noodles to make it healthier. I like to serve with hot dinner rolls.

2 lbs. lean ground turkey	1/4 t. dried thyme
1 c. onions or green onions, chopped	2 bay leaves
	6 to 8 tomatoes, chopped
1/4 c. all-purpose flour	1/4 c. sour cream
1 clove garlic, minced	12-oz. pkg. whole-wheat egg
1 T. paprika	noodles, uncooked and
1 t. salt	divided
1/4 t. pepper	2 t. butter, softened

Brown turkey in a large skillet over medium heat; drain. Add onions and cook until almost tender, stirring well to mix. Blend in flour, garlic and seasonings; mix well. Stir in tomatoes. Reduce heat to low. Cover and simmer, stirring occasionally, until tomatoes are cooked and blended in well, 20 to 30 minutes. Remove from heat and discard bay leaves; stir in sour cream. Meanwhile, cook half of noodles according to package directions; reserve remaining noodles for another recipe. Drain noodles; toss with butter. Serve goulash with hot buttered noodles. Makes 4 to 6 servings.

Food odors will disappear overnight from plastic storage containers if you pack them with crumpled newspaper and secure the lid tightly.

Zucchini & Eggplant over Linguine

Cindy Tropeano
Eastampton, NJ

When my husband had a huge garden, I had to find lots of different ways to use all the veggies! This is a simple, fast, healthy meal that I serve often. We both enjoy it.

16-oz. pkg. linguine pasta, uncooked
2 T. olive oil
1 onion, chopped
2 zucchini, peeled and chopped
2 eggplants, peeled and chopped
3 cloves garlic, chopped
1/4 t. red pepper flakes
salt and pepper to taste
6 tomatoes, diced
Garnish: additional olive oil for drizzling

Cook pasta according to package directions; drain and return to cooking pot. Meanwhile, in a large skillet, heat oil over medium heat. Add onion, zucchini and eggplants; sauté until vegetables are soft. Add garlic and seasonings. Continue to cook for one to 2 minutes. Add tomatoes; use the back of a wooden spoon to mash some of the tomatoes as they cook. Reduce heat to low; simmer another 10 to 15 minutes. Add sauce to pasta and toss; drizzle with a little oil and serve. Makes 4 servings.

Flea markets and yard sales offer an amazing variety of table serving pieces for entertaining! Watch for vintage china, casseroles and jelly-jar glasses to add old-fashioned charm to your dinner table.

Comfort Foods

Judy's Skillet Spaghetti

Judy Schroff
Churubusco, IN

*This was one of my favorite go-to recipes while I was working
and raising a family. It's very simple and uses ingredients
most of us have in our pantries.*

1 lb. ground beef
3 c. water
2-1/4 c. tomato juice
6-oz. can tomato paste
2 T. dried, minced onion
2 T. chili powder

1 t. sugar
1 t. garlic salt
1 t. dried oregano
8-oz. pkg. spaghetti, uncooked
Garnish: grated Parmesan
    cheese

In a large skillet, brown beef over medium heat; drain. Add remaining
ingredients except spaghetti. Cover and bring to a boil. Reduce heat to
low. Simmer for 30 minutes, stirring occasionally. Add uncooked
spaghetti and stir to separate strands. Cover and simmer another
30 minutes, stirring occasionally, or until spaghetti is tender. Serve
sprinkled with grated Parmesan cheese. Makes 6 servings.

Real cloth napkins make mealtime just a little more special...
and they're a must when spaghetti is on the menu! Stitch
fun charms to napkin rings, so everyone can identify
their own napkin easily.

Mexican Chicken Tortilla Casserole

Diane Cohen
Breinigsville, PA

We all love a hearty Mexican casserole! This recipe has been changed up with reduced-fat cheeses and whole-wheat tortillas.

1 lb. boneless, skinless chicken breasts, cut into bite-size pieces
2 t. taco seasoning mix
1 red or green bell pepper, chopped
1-1/2 c. salsa
1/2 c. reduced-fat cream cheese, softened

15-oz. can black beans, drained and rinsed
1 tomato, chopped
2 6-inch whole-wheat flour tortillas
1/2 c. shredded reduced-fat Mexican-blend or Cheddar cheese

Sprinkle chicken with seasoning mix; add to a large skillet sprayed with non-stick vegetable spray. Cook over medium heat, stirring frequently, for 4 minutes. Add pepper and cook for 5 minutes, stirring occasionally. Stir in salsa and cream cheese. Cook and stir until melted and blended. Stir in beans and tomato; remove from heat. Spoon 1/3 of chicken mixture into a sprayed 8"x8" baking pan. Cover with one tortilla; layer with half of remaining chicken mixture and half of cheese. Top with remaining tortilla and chicken mixture. Cover and bake at 375 degrees for about 20 minutes, until heated and bubbling. Uncover; sprinkle with remaining cheese. Bake until cheese has melted, about 5 minutes longer. Makes 4 servings.

Whip up a zippy side dish pronto! Prepare instant rice, using chicken broth instead of water. Stir in a generous dollop of spicy salsa, top with shredded cheese and let stand until the cheese melts.

Food
with
Friends

Baked Artichoke Squares

Ellen Folkman
Crystal Beach, FL

This is a recipe I remember my mom, Jennie Miller, making when I was young. It was popular with her friends and, being a great party hostess, she made it often. When she downsized last year, she handed me folders full of recipes she had collected over the years and I found this one among them. I made the squares recently for a potluck party and, just like years ago, they went very quickly!

2 6-oz. jars marinated artichoke hearts
1/2 c. onion, chopped
1 clove garlic, minced
4 eggs, beaten
1/4 c. dry bread crumbs
1/2 t. fresh Italian parsley, chopped
2 c. shredded Cheddar cheese
salt and pepper to taste

Drain liquid from one jar of artichokes into a skillet; drain liquid from remaining jar and discard. Chop all artichokes and set aside. Heat liquid in skillet over medium heat. Sauté onion and garlic until soft; drain. In a bowl, combine eggs, bread crumbs and parsley. Stir in onion mixture, chopped artichokes, cheese, salt and pepper. Pour mixture into a greased 13"x9" inch baking pan. Bake at 325 degrees for 30 to 35 minutes. Cool; cut into small squares. Serves 8 to 10.

The secret to being a relaxed hostess...choose foods that can be prepared in advance. At party time, simply pull from the fridge and serve, or pop into a hot oven as needed.

Food with Friends

Spinach-Stuffed Mushrooms

Jill Burton
Gooseberry Patch

These mushrooms are scrumptious but just a little lighter than the usual sausage-filled version. Don't toss the mushroom stems... they can be chopped and added to scrambled eggs or burgers.

30 mushroom caps
1 to 2 T. olive oil
1 egg
1 t. garlic, minced
salt and pepper to taste
10-oz. pkg. frozen chopped
    spinach, thawed and very
    well drained

1/4 c. seasoned dry bread
    crumbs
1/4 c. shredded Gouda cheese
1/4 c. shredded mozzarella
    cheese
1/2 c. grated Parmesan cheese,
    divided

Brush mushroom caps with oil on all sides; brush a shallow 13"x9" baking pan lightly with remaining oil. Arrange mushrooms in pan. Bake at 375 degrees until just tender, about 12 minutes. Meanwhile, whisk together egg, garlic, salt and pepper in a bowl. Stir in spinach, bread crumbs, Gouda cheese, mozzarella cheese and 1/4 cup Parmesan cheese. Remove mushrooms from the oven; drain any juices from pan. Spoon spinach mixture into mushrooms; sprinkle with remaining Parmesan cheese. Bake for another 10 minutes, until heated through and golden. Makes 2-1/2 dozen.

Stock up on festive party napkins, candles and table decorations at post-holiday sales. Tuck them away in a big box...you'll be all set to turn a casual get-together into a party.

Cheesy Beer Fondue

Sonya Labbe
West Hollywood, CA

Fondue is great for entertaining! Whenever my parents had people over to visit, they loved serving this fondue. Everybody would take their time to eat and mingle together.

1/2 head cauliflower, separated
   into flowerets
1/2 bunch broccoli, separated
   into flowerets
1 c. shredded Cheddar cheese
1 c. shredded Gruyère cheese
1 c. shredded Swiss cheese
1 T. all-purpose flour
1-1/2 c. favorite beer or
   non-alcoholic beer
2 T. Dijon mustard
1 baguette, cubed

Bring a medium saucepan of water to a boil over high heat. Add cauliflower and broccoli flowerets; boil for 2 minutes and drain. Combine cheeses in a bowl. Sprinkle with flour and toss to coat; set aside. Pour the beer into a small saucepan over medium heat. Bring to a simmer; add cheese mixture in batches, stirring with a wooden spoon until completely blended. Stir in mustard. Transfer cheese mixture to a warm fondue pot; keep warm. To serve, arrange cauliflower, broccoli, and bread cubes around fondue pot. Serves 6.

Prefer to shred cheese yourself? Freeze wrapped cheese for 10 to 20 minutes...it will just glide across the grater!

Food with Friends

Guiltless Queso Dip

Christine Gordon
Sheppard AFB, TX

Our whole family loves queso and chips! We eat it when our family gathers to celebrate birthdays or holidays and especially during football season. With this recipe, we can keep eating one of our favorite snacks...no worries!

1 lb. ground turkey sausage
3 T. butter, sliced
3 T. all-purpose flour
1-1/2 to 2 c. low-fat milk,
    to desired consistency
8-oz. pkg. shredded Monterey
    Jack cheese
10-oz. can diced tomatoes and
    green chiles, drained

salt and pepper to taste
Optional: small amount milk
baked corn tortilla chips
cut fresh vegetables like broccoli
    flowerets, cherry tomatoes,
    snow peas, carrot sticks and
    red and yellow pepper strips

In a large Dutch oven over medium heat, brown and crumble sausage. Drain; remove sausage to a plate and set aside. Melt butter in the same pan over medium heat; sprinkle in flour. Cook and stir for about one minute. Add milk slowly, stirring into butter mixture. Cook, stirring constantly, until mixture begins to thicken; heat through. Add cheese; cook and stir until melted. Add sausage, tomatoes, salt and pepper; stir until heated through. If mixture seems too thick, slowly stir in a small amount of milk to desired consistency. Ladle the hot queso into a serving bowl. Serve with tortilla chips and fresh vegetables for dipping. Serves 8 to 10.

Looking for a new way to serve a favorite snack? Retro-style plates, cake stands and chip & dip sets really add color and fun.

English Rabbit

Karen Mach
Pawlet, VT

This recipe for savory English muffin bites came from a co-worker back in the 1970s. We often take it to parties and everyone requests the recipe. It is always a hit!

1/2 c. mayonnaise
1/2 c. black olives, chopped
1/2 c. onion, chopped

1-1/2 c. shredded Cheddar
   cheese
12 English muffins, split

In a bowl, combine all ingredients except English muffins; mix well. Spread mixture over muffin halves; cut each into quarters. Arrange on an ungreased baking sheet. Place under a preheated boiler; broil until bubbly and golden. Serve warm. Makes 4 dozen.

Add some vintage flair to your buffet by placing gently used game boards under your serving dishes. Check the closet for forgotten games or pick some up at yard sales. Cover with self-adhesive clear plastic for wipe-clean ease.

Food with Friends

Veggie Party Pizza

Sarah Cameron
Maryville, TN

An old favorite! I always make this for a little something extra
to set out at parties. Guests love having a healthy option.
Feel free to mix & match your favorite fresh veggies!

2 8-oz. tubes refrigerated
   crescent rolls
8-oz. pkg. cream cheese,
   softened
1-oz. pkg. ranch salad
   dressing mix

1 c. broccoli flowerets, finely
   chopped
1/2 c. red pepper, finely chopped
1/2 c. carrot, finely chopped

Press crescent rolls into the bottom of a round pizza pan or a baking
sheet, pressing and sealing seams together. Bake at 375 degrees for
10 to 12 minutes, until golden; remove from oven and let cool. In
small bowl, combine cream cheese and dressing mix; stir together
until creamy. Spread cheese mixture evenly over baked crust. Sprinkle
evenly with chopped vegetables. Cut into wedges or squares.
Serves 10.

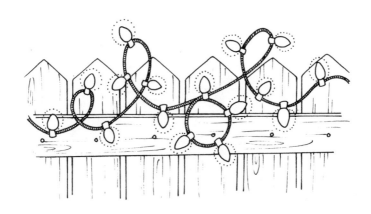

Partying outdoors? Wind sparkling white lights along
the garden fence and in the trees for a twinkling
firefly effect as the sun sets.

Sweet & Spicy Cranberry Spread
Marilyn Morel
Keene, NH

My mom loved to entertain. She always set out a block of cream cheese with a special topping to serve with assorted crackers. This is a holiday version that is so unusual and addictive...pretty too!

8-oz. pkg. cream cheese
1/2 c. whole-berry cranberry
  sauce
1/2 c. red pepper jelly
2 T. sugar
1 T. fresh cilantro, chopped

Optional: 1 small jalapeño
  pepper, seeded and finely
  chopped
Garnish: additional fresh cilantro
assorted crackers

Place cream cheese on a serving plate. Let stand for 15 to 30 minutes at room temperature. Meanwhile, in a small microwave-safe bowl, combine cranberry sauce, jelly and sugar. Microwave, uncovered, on high for about 30 seconds. Stir until sugar is dissolved. Cool slightly; stir in cilantro. Spoon cranberry mixture over cream cheese, allowing mixture to drip down sides of cheese. Sprinkle with jalapeño, if using, and cilantro. Serve with crackers. Makes 8 to 10 servings.

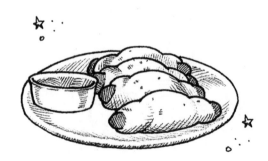

Serve up pigs in a blanket for old-fashioned fun! Unroll crescent rolls and cut each roll lengthwise into 3 narrow triangles. Roll up a cocktail wiener in each triangle and bake at 375 degrees for 11 to 14 minutes. Serve warm with mustard for dipping.

Food with Friends

Cranberry Chicken Salad Bites

Sheri Kohl
Wentzville, MO

A staple at every spring and summer gathering! It's equally good for Mothers' Day, bridal showers or a light lunch on warm summer days.

24 frozen mini pastry shells
4 c. cooked chicken, finely
   chopped
3 stalks celery, diced
1 c. sweetened dried cranberries

1/3 c. chopped pecans
1-1/2 c. mayonnaise
1/3 c. honey, or more to taste
1/4 t. salt
1/4 t. pepper

Bake pastry shells according to package directions; let cool. Meanwhile, in a large bowl, combine chicken, celery, cranberries and pecans. Mix remaining ingredients in a separate bowl; add to chicken mixture and stir gently until combined. Spoon into pastry shells and serve. Makes 2 dozen.

Guests are sure to appreciate pitchers of ice water they can help themselves to. Make some fancy party ice cubes by tucking sprigs of mint into ice cube trays before freezing.

Stuffed Avocados with Shrimp Dip Salad

Wendy Ball
Battle Creek, MI

I love crab rangoon, but one day I didn't have any crab or wonton wrappers on hand, so I substituted shrimp for crab and avocado for the wrappers. This is perfect as either a salad or an appetizer dip to serve with fresh vegetables. You can substitute reduced-fat cream cheese and use canned shrimp in place of frozen shrimp.

8-oz. pkg. cream cheese,
  softened
1/3 c. mayonnaise
1 T. lemon juice
3/4 c. celery, chopped
1/4 c. green onion, chopped

1 c. frozen large shrimp, thawed,
  peeled, cleaned and tails
  removed
4 avocados or assorted cut-up
  vegetables

In a bowl, beat cream cheese, mayonnaise and lemon juice until well blended. Stir in celery, onion and shrimp. Cover; refrigerate for at least one to 2 hours to blend flavors. At serving time, cut avocados in half; remove pits. Scoop 1/4 cup of shrimp salad into each avocado half. Avocado halves may be cut in half once again, for smaller servings. Shrimp salad may also be placed in a serving bowl and served as a dip with fresh vegetables. Makes 8 servings.

Make some wonton crackers for snacking. Separate refrigerated wonton wrappers and cut each in half, forming 2 triangles. Brush lightly on both sides with olive oil and arrange on a baking sheet. Bake at 350 degrees for 5 to 7 minutes, until crisp and golden. Sprinkle warm chips with salt, if you like.

Food with Friends

Creamy Tuna-Walnut Spread

Teri Lindquist
Gurnee, IL

I've been making this wonderful combination of ingredients for many years...everyone raves over it! I found a version in an old cookbook and added my own touches. I especially love making a platter of party rye bread topped with this delicious spread when friends are coming over for lunch or tea.

8-oz. pkg. light cream cheese,
   softened
1/2 c. mayonnaise
6-oz. can water-packed tuna,
   drained and flaked
4-oz. can sliced black olives,
   drained
1/2 c. chopped walnuts or
   pecans

2 T. lemon juice
1 to 2 T. green onion, thinly
   sliced
salt and pepper to taste
party rye bread, croissants,
   crackers, celery and carrot
   sticks

In a bowl, combine all ingredients except bread, crackers and vegetables. Mix well, using an electric mixer on low speed for a smoother texture. Cover and chill. Spread on bread, croissants or crackers, or serve as a dip for vegetables. Makes 8 servings.

Dear Mary,
I'm hosting a dinner party at my home - Friday, December 31st, at eight o'clock.
I do hope you can come. Please call me at (Central 5 - 6407)
Sincerely,
June Swanson

Remember that happy feeling as a kid when a party invitation arrived in the mail? Mail out written invitations to your next get-together, no matter how informal. Your grown-up friends will love it!

Tastes Like Home

Red Pepper Hummus

Terri Steffes
Saint Charles, MO

I started making my own hummus when I learned how inexpensive it was compared to the store-bought kind. Served with fresh veggies, it's a healthy snack.

15-oz. can garbanzo beans,
  drained and rinsed
1 red pepper, roasted and
  seeded, or 1 canned roasted
  red pepper
1 clove garlic, minced
2 T. olive oil

1 T. tahini
3 T. lemon juice
1 t. ground cumin
1 t. salt
1 t. pepper
assorted cut-up vegetables

In a food processor, combine all ingredients except cut-up vegetables in the order listed. Process until beans are a smooth, paste-like consistency. Cover and chill. Serve as a dip with vegetables. Makes 12 servings.

Artichoke-Pepper Dip

Agnes Vona
Highland, NY

A flavorful appetizer everyone can snack on while waiting for other guests to arrive. It goes well with all kinds of beverages.

8-oz. pkg. cream cheese,
  softened
6-oz. jar marinated artichokes,
  drained
12-oz. jar roasted red peppers,
  drained

1 clove garlic, chopped
salt and pepper to taste
1/4 t. red pepper flakes
2 T. olive oil
toasted pita bread, tortilla chips,
  cut-up vegetables

In a food processor, combine all ingredients except oil and pitas, tortilla chips and vegetables. Add oil while processing to a fairly soft consistency. Cover and chill for 30 minutes. Serve with pitas, tortilla chips or vegetables. Makes 10 to 12 servings.

Food with Friends

Karen's Guacamole

Karen Ensign
Providence, UT

A bowl of zesty guacamole is a must when serving Mexican food or just for dipping into with crisp tortilla chips. You'll love mine!

3 avocados, halved, pitted
   and cubed
juice of 1 lime
1/2 c. tomato, diced

1/4 c. red onion, diced
1/3 c. fresh cilantro, chopped
salt to taste
tortilla chips

Add avocados to a bowl; drizzle with lime juice. Mix in tomato, onion and cilantro; season with salt. Serve with tortilla chips. Serves 6.

Avocado Ranch Dip

Michelle Corriveau
Blackstone, MA

I was looking for something tasty with a lot of protein to bring to get-togethers and this is what I came up with. It's absolutely delicious as a dip...it even makes a great sandwich spread!

2 avocados, halved, pitted
   and cubed
1-oz. pkg. ranch salad dressing
   mix

1 c. low-fat plain Greek yogurt
cut-up vegetables or tortilla
   chips

In a bowl, mash avocados until nearly smooth. Add dressing mix and yogurt; stir until blended. Cover and chill. Serve with vegetables or tortilla chips. Serves 6.

Freeze mashed, fresh avocado to keep on hand. Just add
1/2 teaspoon of lime or lemon juice per avocado, mix well
and store in a plastic zipping bag, making sure to remove
all the air before sealing. Thaw in the refrigerator.

Baked Homestyle French Fries
Anne Ptacnik
Yuma, CO

These hot-from-the-oven fries are a staple in our family. My three young kids love them alongside burgers from the grill. We think they taste just as good as the fried version!

4 russet potatoes, sliced into
    thin strips
3 to 4 T. oil
garlic powder, salt and pepper
    to taste

2 T. grated Parmesan cheese
Garnish: catsup or barbecue
    sauce

Arrange potatoes in a single layer on a baking sheet. Drizzle with oil; sprinkle with seasonings and Parmesan cheese. Toss with hands. Bake at 400 degrees for 20 minutes, or to desired crispness, occasionally turning fries with a spatula for even baking. Serve hot with catsup or barbecue sauce. Makes 4 to 6 servings.

Serve sliders at your next party...everyone will love them!
Mix up your favorite meatball recipe, then form the mixture
into flattened mini burgers. Pan-fry or bake as desired
and serve on mini sandwich buns.

Food with Friends

Zucchini Fries

Beverley Williams
San Antonio, TX

This recipe came about when I wanted a tasty, healthy alternative to French fries. My kids love them and don't mind eating their veggies!

4 zucchini, peeled and halved
   lengthwise
1 c. dry bread crumbs
1/3 c. grated Parmesan cheese
1 T. dried basil

1 t. dried oregano
1/4 t. seasoned salt
1/8 t. garlic powder
1/4 c. butter, melted

Line a baking sheet with aluminum foil; spray lightly with non-stick vegetable spray and set aside. Cut each zucchini half lengthwise into 4 strips; set aside. In a shallow dish, combine bread crumbs, Parmesan cheese and seasonings; mix well. Add melted butter to a separate shallow dish. Dip each zucchini strip into melted butter; dredge in crumb mixture to coat. Shake off any excess. Place zucchini strips in a single layer on baking sheet. Bake at 425 degrees for 15 minutes, or until tender and golden. Makes 6 servings.

Looking for a new family message board? Hang an old-fashioned washboard for a whimsical way to keep notes organized. Just use magnets to keep messages and photos secure.

Bobbie's Hawaiian Chicken Wings

Bobbie Metzger
Pittsburgh, PA

I'm always asked to bring these yummy wings to parties! Being born in Hawaii, this recipe is dear to my heart. It has been in my family for as long as I can remember. For the best results, be sure to start the night before.

3 lbs. chicken wings, separated
1 c. all-purpose flour
1/2 c. soy sauce
6 T. sugar

6 cloves garlic, pressed
1/2-inch slice fresh ginger,
    peeled and grated
oil for deep frying

The night before, coat chicken wings with flour and place in a large bowl. In a small bowl, combine remaining ingredients except oil. Cover both bowls; refrigerate overnight. The next day, add 2 to 3 inches oil to a large heavy stockpot (just enough oil to cover wings). Heat oil over medium-high heat to about 350 degrees. Working in batches, add wings to oil. Cook for 13 to 14 minutes, until crisp and golden. Drain on paper towels; remove to a serving platter. Stir soy sauce mixture again. Immediately spoon soy sauce mixture over wings, coating well. Serve immediately. Makes about 3 dozen.

Coat lots of chicken wings at once, the no-mess way. Just add
the flour or coating mix to a large plastic zipping bag,
drop in the wings, seal the bag and shake to coat them.
Afterwards, just toss away the bag.

Lighter Buffalo Wings

Cindy Neel
Gooseberry Patch

My family just loves buffalo wings when we're tailgating or watching football on TV, but lately we've been watching what we eat. These boneless tenders are super flavorful and a little healthier than regular wings...they scored a touchdown with everyone!

3 lbs. chicken tenders
1/2 c. plus 2 T. hot pepper
    sauce, divided
1/4 c. white vinegar
2 T. fresh oregano, chopped

1 T. garlic powder
1 T. chili powder
4 t. paprika
salt and pepper to taste
Garnish: celery sticks

Place chicken tenders in a large dish. In a separate bowl, mix 2 tablespoons hot sauce, vinegar and seasonings; drizzle over wings. Mix well; cover and refrigerate for 30 minutes. Arrange tenders on a broiler pan and broil for about 10 minutes per side, or until golden and juices run clear. Heat remaining hot sauce until warm; toss with tenders. Serve with Light Blue Cheese Dressing and celery sticks. Makes about 3 dozen.

Light Blue Cheese Dressing:

1/2 c. plain Greek yogurt
1/2 c. crumbled blue cheese
3 T. mayonnaise
2 T. cider vinegar

1 T. olive oil
salt and pepper to taste
1/4 t. dry mustard
Optional: buttermilk to taste

In a bowl, combine all ingredients except buttermilk; blend well. Thin with buttermilk, if desired. Cover and chill. Makes 2 cups.

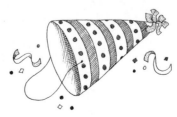

One cannot have too large a party.
–Jane Austen

Tex-Mex Dip

Mary Ann Dimick
Bowling Green, OH

I first tasted this recipe years ago at a birthday party hosted by my mother-in-law. I knew my co-workers would love it, so I made it for our next potluck. It was a huge hit, and was requested from then on for any work-related functions. My family likes it too...my daughter-in-law always requests it for her birthday dinner.

3 avocados, halved, pitted
   and cubed
3 T. lemon juice
salt and pepper to taste
1 c. light sour cream
1/2 c. mayonnaise
1-1/4 oz. pkg. taco seasoning
   mix

16-oz. can fat-free refried beans
2 to 3 tomatoes, chopped
1/2 c. onion, chopped
4-oz. can sliced black olives,
   drained
8-oz. pkg. shredded Mexican-
   blend or mild Cheddar cheese
tortilla chips

In a large bowl, mash avocados with lemon juice, salt and pepper; set aside. In a small bowl, mix sour cream, mayonnaise and taco seasoning; set aside. Spread refried beans in the bottom of a 13"x9" glass baking pan. Layer with avocado mixture, sour cream mixture, tomatoes, onion, olives and cheese. Cover and chill until serving time. Serve with tortilla chips. Serves 10 to 12.

Tuck packets of gravy and seasoning mix into a vintage napkin holder to keep the pantry tidy.

Food with Friends

Lori's Fresh Salsa

Lori Braegelmann
Saint Cloud, MN

The best salsa ever! I make this salsa every week year 'round...every batch is good! It's made with canned tomatoes but tastes so fresh. Feel free to add more or less cilantro and red pepper flakes to your own taste. Enjoy with tortilla chips, tacos, scrambled eggs and whatever you like.

2 14-1/2 oz. cans petite diced
   tomatoes, divided
4-oz. can diced green chiles
1 to 2 jalapeño peppers, seeded
   and chopped
1/3 c. fresh cilantro, chopped

1/2 white onion, chopped
6 green onions, chopped
1 to 2 wedges lime
1/4 t. red pepper flakes
salt and pepper to taste

Add one can tomatoes with juice and green chiles to a blender. Process for about 5 seconds; do not overblend. Transfer to a bowl; add second can of tomatoes with juice, jalapeños, cilantro and onions. Mix lightly. Squeeze in lime juice; add seasonings. Cover and chill for one hour before serving. Keep refrigerated up to one week. Makes about 4 cups.

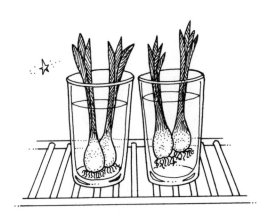

Keep green onions fresh longer by storing them bulb-ends
down in a half-full glass of water in the refrigerator.
Change the water every few days.

Hot Corn Dip

Teresa Moore
Pawhuska, OK

*I make this colorful dip for holidays. It's super-easy to
stir up and makes enough for a large party.*

8-oz. pkg. cream cheese,
  softened
15-oz. can yellow corn, drained
15-oz. can shoepeg corn,
  drained

14-1/2 oz. can diced tomatoes
  with green chiles, drained
1/2 t. chili powder
1/2 t. garlic powder
scoop-type corn chips

In a large bowl, blend together all ingredients except corn chips. Spread
in an ungreased 8"x8" baking pan. Bake, uncovered, at 350 degrees
for 30 minutes, or until hot and bubbly. Serve warm with corn chips.
Makes about 6 cups.

A dip buffet will be fun at your next get-together! Have plenty of
chips, crackers, sliced veggies, bread rounds and pita triangles
on hand. Get creative and serve your dips in unexpected serving
"dishes" such as hollowed-out vegetables and breads.

Food with Friends

Linda's Mexican Dip

Renee Johnson
Cookeville, TN

This is a quick & easy recipe that my mom made over the years. Everyone seems to love it, and you can't believe how easy it is to make! If you have any leftovers (we rarely do!) it reheats well.

8-oz. pkg. cream cheese
1 c. salsa, or more to taste
1-1/2 c. shredded Cheddar or
    Mexican-blend cheese

scoop-type tortilla chips
    or corn chips

Place unwrapped cream cheese in an ungreased microwave-safe 8"x8" glass baking pan. Microwave for about one minute, until soft; spread in pan. Top with salsa and cheese. Microwave for 2 minutes, or until cheese melts. Serve warm with tortilla chips. Makes 9 to 12 servings.

Joni's Salsa

Joan Bitting
Papillion, NE

I serve this at gatherings any time of the year. Everyone loves it, even kids!

3 to 4 ripe tomatoes, or
    10 to 15 roma tomatoes,
    diced
1 onion, chopped

1 T. salsa verde
2 t. salt
1/2 c. fresh cilantro, chopped
tortilla chips

In a bowl, combine all ingredients except tortilla chips. Stir gently. Serve as a topping or as a dip with tortilla chips. Makes 3 cups.

Scoop out the centers of cherry tomatoes, then fill with a dollop of a flavorful, creamy spread. Lighter than crackers and chips...so pretty on an appetizer tray too!

Beau Monde Bread Bowl Dip

Jessica Kraus
Delaware, OH

This dip takes me back to my childhood! Whenever we had a party, this is the dip my mom always made. I still love it. The longer the dip is refrigerated, the better it will taste, so it's best to make it the night before.

1-1/4 c. sour cream	1 T. Beau Monde seasoning
1-1/4 c. mayonnaise	1 t. dill weed
6-oz. jar dried beef, chopped	1 round loaf pumpernickel bread
1 T. onion, chopped	cut-up vegetables

In a bowl, combine all ingredients except bread and vegetables; mix well. Cover and chill for at least one hour to overnight. At serving time, hollow out bread bowl, reserving bread pieces. Spoon dip into bread bowl. Serve with bread pieces and vegetables. Serves 8.

Lightly cook or blanch vegetables to keep them brightly colored...perfect for a dipping platter. Simply drop the trimmed veggies into a pan of boiling water and cook briefly until tender, then immerse in ice water and drain.

Food with Friends

Festive Pimento Cheese

April Garner
Independence, KY

Scrumptious! This spread is also great made with extra-sharp Cheddar cheese or even reduced-fat Cheddar for a few less calories. Sometimes we add a few sliced olives for a little different taste.

8-oz. pkg. Vermont white
    Cheddar cheese, grated
1/2 c. light mayonnaise,
    or to taste

2-oz. jar diced pimentos, drained
party rye bread, crackers or
    tortilla chips

Place cheese in a bowl. Add mayonnaise and mix to desired consistency; fold in pimentos. Cover and chill. Serve with bread, crackers or tortilla chips. Makes 10 servings.

Swap party specialties with a friend! For example, offer to trade a kettle of your super-secret-recipe chili for a dozen or two of your best girlfriend's fabulous cupcakes. It's a super way to save party-planning time and money.

Swiss Cheese & Olive Spread

Gladys Kielar
Whitehouse, OH

Bring a new appetizer to the next party you attend!
This is a favorite of ours that you'll love too.

3 c. shredded Swiss cheese
3-oz. pkg. cream cheese, cubed
1/4 c. dry white wine or chicken
   broth
3 T. mayonnaise
1 t. Worcestershire sauce
3 T. fresh parsley, snipped

1/3 c. chopped black olives,
   drained
3 T. green onions, finely
   chopped
snack crackers or party rye
   bread

Place cheeses in a large bowl; cover and let stand for 30 minutes at room temperature. Add wine or broth, mayonnaise and Worcestershire sauce. Beat with an electric mixer on low speed until blended. Stir in parsley, olives and onions. Transfer to a serving bowl; cover and chill for at least 2 hours. Let stand at room temperature for one hour before serving. Serve with crackers or bread. Makes 10 servings.

Primitive-style wooden cutting boards in fun shapes like pigs, fish or roosters can often be found at tag sales. Put them to use as whimsical party snack servers.

Food with Friends

Brenna's Cheese Ball

Brenna Schiffhauer
Alexander, NC

A family favorite, passed down from generation to generation

1-1/2 c. cream cheese, softened
1/4 c. mayonnaise
1/2 t. Italian seasoning
1/8 t. garlic powder

1/3 c. grated Parmesan cheese
Garnish: chopped nuts,
   1 maraschino cherry
snack crackers

In a large bowl, combine cream cheese, mayonnaise, seasonings and Parmesan cheese. Blend well and form into a ball, then roll in nuts and top with cherry. Wrap in plastic; chill 8 hours to overnight. Serve with crackers. Serves 6 to 8.

A super-simple tip when cooking with cream cheese! An 8-ounce package equals one cup, so when a recipe calls for 1/2 cup cream cheese, just cut the package in half. No measuring cup to wash!

Ginger Cocktail Sausages

Janis Parr
Ontario, Canada

This simple recipe makes delicious homemade mini sausages to serve at any get-together. I guarantee you will be asked for the recipe!

2 egg yolks
1 lb. ground pork sausage
1/2 c. dill pickle, chopped

1 t. ground ginger
2 T. all-purpose flour

Beat egg yolks in a large bowl. Add sausage, pickle and ginger, blending well. Cover and chill for 2 to 3 hours. Form into small sausages, about one inch long and 1/2-inch in diameter, or to desired size. Roll each sausage in flour. Cook sausages in a skillet over medium heat, turning occasionally until lightly browned and cooked through. Serve warm. Makes about 4 dozen.

No-Guilt Dijon Mustard Dip

Becky Drees
Pittsfield, MA

This tastes a lot like traditional sour cream & onion dip, but with less fat. Great with fresh broccoli flowerets, cherry tomatoes, sliced apple, fennel or celery sticks.

1 c. fat-free plain Greek yogurt
1/4 c. light mayonnaise
4 t. Dijon mustard

4 t. fresh chives or green onions, minced
baked potato chips

In a bowl, stir together yogurt, mayonnaise, mustard and chives or onions. Cover and chill. May be kept refrigerated 2 to 3 days. Serve with potato chips. Serves 4.

Soft pretzel bites in a jiffy! Cut refrigerated bread sticks into short lengths. Sprinkle with coarse salt, bake as the package directs and serve warm.

Food with Friends

Ronnie's Smokies

Judy Cooper
Cookeville, TN

A dear friend from years ago shared this recipe and it's been a hit every single time it's served.

16-oz. pkg. frozen meatballs
14-oz. pkg. mini cocktail
    sausages
20-oz. can pineapple chunks,
    drained

4-oz. can sliced mushrooms,
    drained
8-oz. bottle Catalina or French
    salad dressing

Combine all ingredients in a lightly greased 13"x9" baking pan; stir gently. Cover and bake at 350 degrees for about one hour, until hot and bubbly. Serves 8 to 12.

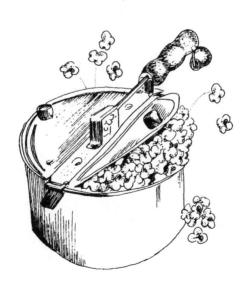

For a quick & easy snack that everybody loves, nothing beats a big bowl of popcorn. Jazz it up with a sprinkle of grated Parmesan cheese or taco seasoning mix, or serve it the classic way, with butter and salt.

Chicken Meatballs

Stephanie Gegg
Sainte Genevieve, MO

Serve these tasty meatballs with your favorite pasta and sauce for a delicious dinner, or with toothpicks for parties. Just 25 calories and one gram of fat per meatball!

1-1/4 lbs. ground chicken breast
1 egg, beaten
1/4 c. fat-free milk
2/3 c. Italian-seasoned dry
   bread crumbs
1/2 c. grated Parmesan cheese

1-1/2 t. dried parsley
1 t. salt
1/4 t. seasoning salt
1/4 t. pepper
1/4 t. onion powder
1/4 t. garlic powder

In a large bowl, combine all ingredients. Mix with your hands just until combined; do not overmix. Form into 1-1/2 inch balls. Place on a lightly greased baking sheet. Bake at 350 degrees for 16 minutes, or until cooked through. Makes 2 to 2-1/2 dozen.

An old-fashioned food grinder is handy for grinding meat for recipes. To clean it easily when you've finished, just put a half-slice of bread through the grinder. The bread will remove any food particles.

Food with Friends

Healthy Fried Chicken Nuggets

Teresa Eller
Kansas City, KS

If your family loves crispy chicken nuggets,
this recipe is for you.

1 c. whole-wheat flour
1/4 c. milled flax seed
2 t. dried, minced onion
1 t. garlic powder

4 boneless, skinless chicken
    breasts, cubed
1/4 c. extra-virgin olive oil

In a one-gallon plastic zipping bag, combine flour, flax seed, onion and garlic powder; mix well. Place chicken cubes in bag; seal and shake bag to coat. Heat oil in a skillet over medium heat. Add chicken; cook for about 8 minutes on each side, or until juices run clear. Drain on paper towels. Serves 6.

Whip up a delicious honey-mustard dip for chicken nuggets with 2/3 cup honey and 1/3 cup mustard. Try different kinds of honey and mustard to create flavor variations.

Microwave Bread & Butter Pickles *Janet Sharp*
Milford, OH

A really quick & easy recipe for bread & butter pickles without canning. They taste as good as home-canned!

1 c. white vinegar	1 t. mustard seed
1 c. sugar or calorie-free powdered sweetener	1/2 t. celery seed
	1/2 t. turmeric
1/2 c. water	2-3/4 to 3 lbs. cucumbers, sliced
2 t. salt	1/8-inch to 1/4-inch thick
1 t. dried, minced garlic	1 onion, thinly sliced

In a large microwave-safe bowl, combine vinegar, sugar or sweetener, water, salt and seasonings. Stir well. Add cucumbers and onions; mix gently. Microwave, uncovered, on high for 9 minutes, stirring every 3 minutes. Remove from microwave and allow to cool, reserving liquid with pickles. Cover and refrigerate overnight. Place pickles in jars; add enough of the liquid to cover. Be sure to distribute liquid evenly if using more than one jar. Store in refrigerator or freezer. Makes about 8 cups.

English cucumbers are uniformly shaped and have very few seeds...a great choice for pickles. If you choose the waxy American variety, be sure to peel away the skin and remove any tough seeds.

Food with Friends

Spicy Baked Radish Chips

Ava Broadwell
Fuquay Varina, NC

We grow lots & lots of radishes in our garden during spring and summer. This is a simple way to use up quite a few radishes, not to mention a tasty low-calorie snack.

8 to 10 radishes
2 t. olive oil
1/2 t. sriracha hot chili sauce,
   or to taste

2 cloves garlic, minced
1 t. sugar
1/2 t. white wine vinegar
Optional: salt to taste

Slice radishes paper-thin using a mandoline or paring knife; set aside in a large bowl. In a small bowl, combine remaining ingredients except salt. Whisk very well until blended. Add mixture to radishes; toss to coat and let stand at least 30 minutes. Drain radishes; spread on a baking sheet that has been sprayed with non-stick vegetable spray. Bake at 375 degrees for about 10 minutes, turning radishes over after 5 minutes. Sprinkle with salt, if desired. Serves 2.

For a fruit-studded ice ring that won't dilute your party punch bowl, arrange sliced oranges, lemons and limes in a ring mold. Pour in a small amount of punch and freeze. Repeat this process until the mold is filled; dip in hot water to release.

Caramelized Onion & Roasted Garlic Dip

Jasmine Burgess
East Lansing, MI

My husband loves chips & dip, so I came up with this dip that's rich and creamy tasting, yet light in fat and calories. It takes a little time, but it's delicious and great for parties. I like to serve it with fresh veggies and whole-grain crackers.

1-1/2 yellow or sweet onions, sliced
2 t. extra-virgin olive oil
2 t. salt, divided
Optional: 1/4 c. chicken broth or water

1 c. plain low-fat Greek yogurt
1/2 c. light mayonnaise
1 t. dill weed
1 t. dried thyme
Optional: 1/2 t. smoked sea salt

Heat oil in a large skillet over medium heat. Add onions and one teaspoon salt. Sauté, stirring occasionally, for 20 to 30 minutes, until onions are a dark golden caramel color and have cooked down to about 1/2 cup. Add broth or water as needed to keep onions from drying out. Remove from heat; cool until onions are just warm to the touch. In a food processor, combine onions, Roasted Garlic and remaining ingredients. Process until well combined. Season with more salt, if needed. Serve immediately, or cover and chill until serving time. Makes 8 to 10 servings.

Roasted Garlic:

1 whole head garlic

1 t. extra-virgin olive oil

Slice the top off garlic head, exposing the cloves. Set garlic on a sheet of aluminum foil and drizzle with oil; wrap in foil. Bake at 400 degrees for 30 minutes. Let cool; press cloves out of their husks and they are ready to use.

It's just as easy to roast 2 heads of garlic as one...why not make an extra to stir into your next batch of mashed potatoes?

Food with Friends

Best Deviled Eggs

Esther Bair
Churubusco, IN

Great-Grandma always garnished her deviled eggs
with a dash of paprika and a slice of olive.

6 to 8 eggs
2 T. mayonnaise, or more to
  taste

1/2 t. mustard
2 t. sugar
1 t. vinegar

Place eggs in a large saucepan; cover generously with water. Bring to
a low boil over high heat. Reduce heat to a simmer; simmer for
18 minutes. Drain water from pan. Cover eggs with cold water,
shaking pan to crack eggshells. Drain; repeat 2 to 3 times. Peel eggs;
cut in half lengthwise and remove yolks. Mash yolks with a fork,
breaking up any chunks. Mix all ingredients into yolks until smooth
and well combined, adding more mayonnaise if a creamier consistency
is desired. Spoon filling into egg whites. Chill. Makes 12 to 16.

Avocado Deviled Eggs

Sarah Cameron
Maryville, TN

A different twist on an old favorite, a little healthier and oh-so easy!

6 eggs, hard-boiled, peeled
  and halved
1 avocado, halved, pitted
  and cubed

1 t. lemon juice
salt and pepper to taste

Cut eggs in half lengthwise; scoop out yolks into a bowl. Place egg
whites on a platter; set aside. In a bowl, mash egg yolks with
remaining ingredients. Spoon filling into egg whites. Chill. Makes one
dozen.

If you're making hard-boiled eggs, use eggs that have been
refrigerated at least 7 to 10 days, instead of fresher eggs.
The shells will slip right off!

Tastes Like Home

Beverley's Fruity Festive Party Punch

Lisa Ann DiNunzio
Vineland, NJ

My mom has made this recipe so many times that I've lost count. It's a true party favorite and tastes so good! It's fun to garnish too. Just before serving, you can float plastic Christmas poinsettias, rubber ducks for a baby shower or edible flowers for a wedding.

8 c. cranberry-grape juice or fruit punch, chilled and divided
2 2-ltr. bottles lemon-lime soda, chilled and divided
1/2 gal. rainbow sherbet, divided

Pour 4 cups of fruit juice and one bottle of soda into a large punch bowl. Add 5 to 7 scoops of sherbet. As the punch bowl gets low, add remaining juice, soda and more scoops of sherbet. Makes 15 to 20 servings.

Cold Coffee Punch

Tammy Epperson
Nancy, KY

Great for weddings, Christmas parties or any occasion! It's a real time-saver since the base can be made ahead of time.

1-1/2 c. hot water
1 c. sugar
1/4 c. instant coffee granules
4 c. whole milk
1/4 c. chocolate syrup
1-1/2 t. vanilla extract
1/2 gal. vanilla ice cream, softened

In a bowl or pitcher, combine hot water, sugar and coffee granules. Stir until dissolved; let cool. Add milk, chocolate syrup and vanilla. Chill. If desired, freeze mixture until ready to serve. To serve, add coffee mixture to a punch bowl; add ice cream and stir gently. Makes 25 servings.

Timeless
Treats

Pat's Easy Strawberry Trifle

Pat Martin
Riverside, CA

I've made this recipe for at least 30 years and came up with it when I wanted to make a quick & easy, but impressive dessert. Everyone wants the recipe! Other soft fruit may be added along with the strawberries. If doubling the recipe, use a large punch bowl.

2 to 3 10-oz. frozen pound cakes or angel food cakes, sliced 3/4-inch thick
2 c. 1% milk
1-oz. pkg. instant sugar-free vanilla pudding mix

1 t. vanilla or almond extract
8-oz. container low-fat frozen whipped topping, thawed
3 10-oz. pkgs. frozen strawberries in sweetened juice, thawed

Arrange cake slices to line the bottom of a straight-sided glass bowl, trimming slices to fit as needed. Set aside bowl and remaining cake. In a separate bowl, combine milk and dry pudding mix; whisk one to 2 minutes, until well blended. Stir in extract; fold in whipped topping. To assemble, layer 1/3 each of strawberries and pudding. Repeat, making 2 more layers of cake, strawberries and pudding. Spread top layer of pudding to edges of bowl. Cover and chill for 2 hours to overnight. Flavor is best when strawberry juices have had time to be absorbed by the cake. Makes 8 servings.

Turn a pretty sugar bowl into a sweet flower vase. Slip a block of floral foam inside and arrange short-stemmed marigolds or zinnias in the foam. Perfect for a dessert table!

Timeless Treats

Cynthia's Impossibly E-Z Cheesecake

Cynthia Dodge
Layton, UT

*I took an original recipe and lightened up the calories
and fat...it's still scrumptious!*

2 8-oz. pkgs. reduced-fat cream
   cheese, cubed and softened
3/4 c. 2% milk
1 c. sugar
1/2 c. reduced-fat biscuit
   baking mix

2 t. vanilla extract
Optional: 2 drops yellow food
   coloring
21-oz. can favorite fruit pie
   filling, or favorite sliced
   fresh fruit

In a large bowl, combine all ingredients except pie filling or fruit. Beat
well with an electric mixer on high speed for 2 minutes, until smooth.
Place a well greased 9" deep-dish pie plate on a baking sheet to catch
any drips. Spoon cream cheese mixture into pie plate. Bake at
350 degrees for 40 to 45 minutes, until center is set. Cool. Top with
pie filling or fresh fruit as desired. Makes 8 servings.

Whip up some homemade cherry pie filling in no time.
Just combine one pound pitted tart cherries, 3/4 cup sugar,
1/3 cup cornstarch and 2 tablespoons lemon juice in a
saucepan over medium heat. Bring to a boil, then simmer
until thickened...so simple!

Raspberry Pretzel Salad

Lou Ann Peterson
Ashville, NY

A quick, delicious dessert! It's a variation of an old recipe with a pretzel bottom crust, but my family likes the crust on top because it doesn't get soggy. You can use sugar-free gelatin mix, fat-free whipped topping and pretzels, and no-calorie powdered sweetener instead of sugar. Strawberries, mixed berries or other seasonal fruit may be used. I use a glass dish so you can see the pretty layers.

2 c. boiling water
2 3-oz. pkgs. raspberry
   gelatin mix
2 c. fresh or frozen raspberries
8-oz. pkg. cream cheese,
   softened

1 c. sugar, divided
8-oz. container frozen whipped
   topping, thawed
1-1/2 c. pretzels, crushed
3 T. butter, melted

Combine boiling water and dry gelatin mix in a 13"x9" glass baking pan; stir until gelatin is dissolved. Stir in raspberries; cover and refrigerate until gelatin is set. Meanwhile, in a large bowl, beat cream cheese with an electric mixer on medium speed, slowly adding 2/3 cup sugar. Beat until creamy. Stir whipped topping into cream cheese mixture; spoon over gelatin layer. In a small bowl, combine crushed pretzels and remaining sugar. Add melted butter; stir well. Sprinkle pretzel mixture over cream cheese mixture. Cover and refrigerate for at least one hour. To serve, cut into squares. Makes 16 servings.

To keep a chilled dessert cool on a warm day, just fill a picnic basket with plastic zipping bags full of ice, lay a colorful tea towel over the ice and set the sweets on top.

Timeless Treats

Lemonade Cheesecake Pie

Nancy Hanson
Murrietta, CA

*I have been making this delicious pie for many years now,
especially when I want to slim down a bit. It is really so light
and delicious...perfect after a heavy meal!*

8-oz. pkg. fat-free cream
  cheese, softened
1 t. sugar-free lemonade
  drink mix
1/2 c. fat-free milk

8-oz. container fat-free frozen
  whipped topping, thawed
9-inch reduced-fat graham
  cracker crust

In a large bowl, beat cream cheese and drink mix with an electric
mixer on medium speed until smooth. Gradually add milk, beating
until well blended. Gently stir in whipped topping; spoon into crust.
Cover and refrigerate for 4 hours, or until firm. Serves 6 to 8.

Spend an afternoon with your mom, learning how to make
the delicious dessert she's always been famous for. Be sure
to have a pad & pen handy to write down every step and
a camera to take some snapshots. Afterwards, sample it
together along with cups of steamy hot tea or coffee.

Aunt Marge's Special Blueberry Dessert

Mary Warren
Sanford, MI

This is an old recipe I remember my aunt making. It is so delicious, I still make it today with blueberries or peaches or both. My family loves it. Try it warm with a scoop of ice cream...yum!

2 c. blueberries
3 T. lemon juice
3 T. butter, softened
1-1/2 c. sugar, divided
1/4 t. salt
1 c. all-purpose flour

1 t. baking powder
1/2 c. milk
Optional: 1/2 t. cinnamon
1 T. cornstarch
1 c. boiling water

Place blueberries in a lightly greased 9"x9" baking pan; drizzle with lemon juice and set aside. In a large bowl, blend together butter, 3/4 cup sugar and salt; set aside. In a separate bowl, mix together flour and baking powder. Add flour mixture and milk alternately to butter mixture; stir well. Pour batter over blueberries; sprinkle with cinnamon, if desired. In a small bowl, combine cornstarch and remaining sugar; sprinkle over top. Pour boiling water over top. Bake at 350 degrees for 45 minutes, or until golden on top. Serves 6.

Fresh-picked berries are a special country pleasure. Store them in a colander in the refrigerator to let cold air circulate around them. Wash them when you're ready to use them.

Yummy Plum Dumplings

Janis Parr
Ontario, Canada

This is a scrumptious dessert. So good served warm with a scoop
of vanilla ice cream. Canned plums may be substituted for fresh...
use their juice as part of the water called for.

4 c. red plums, halved and pitted
4 c. all-purpose flour
1 T. baking powder
1 t. salt
2 c. milk
3 to 4 c. water
1/4 c. butter, diced
1-1/2 c. sugar

Arrange plum halves in a lightly greased 13"x9" baking pan; set aside.
In a bowl, combine flour, baking powder, salt and milk; stir until a soft
dough forms. Lightly pat dough evenly over plums. Pour enough
water down the side of the dough to reach just below the top of the
dough. Dot with butter; sprinkle with sugar. Bake, uncovered,
at 350 degrees for 1-1/2 hours. Serve warm. Makes 8 servings.

Try sugar-substitute blends made especially for baking to
turn out sweet, golden, moist goodies with half the sugar.
There's even a brown sugar variety! Be sure to check
the package for how to measure correctly.

Key Lime Pie

Linda Levitan
Asheville, NC

This is a recipe I have used for many years. I have worked in bakeries since 1965 making various pastries, and Key lime has always been a family favorite. In 1975, when I lived in West Palm Beach, Florida, I was blessed with a Key lime tree in my yard. I have made this pie ahead of time to serve...days later it is still so delicious.

8-oz. pkg. cream cheese,
  softened
1/4 c. sugar
14-oz. can sweetened condensed
  milk

1/2 c. Key lime juice
9-inch pie crust, baked
Garnish: whipped cream, lime
  slices, toasted almonds

In a bowl, beat cream cheese with an electric mixer on medium speed until soft. Add sugar; beat until sugar is dissolved. Beat in condensed milk, then lime juice. Pour filling into baked pie crust. Cover and refrigerate for 3 to 4 hours. Garnish slices with whipped cream, lime slices and almonds. Makes 8 to 10 servings.

When garnishing with lemon or lime slices, do it with a twist!
Cut thin slices with a paring knife, then cut from the center
to the edge. Hold edges and twist in opposite directions.

Timeless Treats

Fresh Strawberry Pie

Judy Beal
Dover, OH

This makes a beautiful pie. It's so easy and one of the best recipes I've tried in more than 50 years! This pie freezes well too.

1 c. water
3/4 c. sugar
1 T. cornstarch
3-oz. pkg. strawberry gelatin
   mix

4 c. fresh strawberries, hulled
   and sliced
9-inch pie crust, baked

In a saucepan, stir water, sugar and cornstarch over medium heat until sugar dissolves. Bring to a boil; cook and stir for 2 minutes, or until thickened. Remove from heat. Stir in dry gelatin mix until dissolved; cool slightly. Arrange strawberries in baked pie crust. Pour cooled gelatin mixture over berries. Cover and refrigerate until set. Makes 6 to 8 servings.

Frozen Lemonade Pie

Beckie Apple
Grannis, AR

Nothing hits the spot on a hot summer day like an icy cold glass of lemonade...unless it would be a slice of this pie! I started making it when our son was little and now he's grown. We never get tired of it. If wrapped tightly in plastic wrap and then placed in a zip-top bag it keeps in the freezer for up 3 months.

16-oz. can frozen lemonade
   concentrate
14-oz. can sweetened condensed
   milk

12-oz. container frozen whipped
   topping, thawed
9-inch graham cracker crust

Combine frozen lemonade and condensed milk in a large bowl. Beat by hand until well blended. Fold in whipped topping. Spoon into crust. Cover and freeze for 2 hours before serving. Serves 8.

Lazy-Day Peach Cobbler

Sandy Pittman
Granby, MO

When I was growing up, this dessert was a welcome treat that smelled wonderful as we came through the door after school. Everyone thinks you went to a lot of trouble, but it's simple to make. I like to top each serving with a spoonful of vanilla ice cream.

1 c. self-rising flour
1 c. sugar
1 t. cinnamon
1/2 t. nutmeg
1/2 c. milk

2 29-oz. cans sliced peaches, drained and 1/2 c. juice reserved
2 t. vanilla extract
1/4 c. butter, melted

In a bowl, mix together flour, sugar and spices; set aside. In a separate bowl, combine milk, reserved peach juice, vanilla and melted butter. Stir well and add to flour mixture. Pour batter into a lightly greased 13"x9" baking pan. Arrange peach slices evenly over batter. Bake at 350 degrees for 45 minutes to one hour, until top and bottom are lightly golden. Let cool about 15 minutes; spoon into dessert bowls. Makes 8 servings.

An old-fashioned cake or pie auction makes a great fundraiser. Tuck each treat in a decorated box and let the bidding begin!

Timeless Treats

My Mom's Apple Crisp

Nancy Girard
Chesapeake, VA

I love my mother's apple crisp...the topping gets so crunchy and yummy! It's different from most crisp recipes since it doesn't call for oats in the topping. Whenever we had been sick and started to feel better, Mom would make us an apple crisp. I always use McIntosh apples because I like the apples to really cook down, almost like applesauce.

4 c. McIntosh apples, peeled,
    cored and sliced
1/4 c. water
1 t. cinnamon
3/4 c. all-purpose flour

1 c. sugar
1/3 c. butter, softened
Garnish: whipped cream or
    vanilla ice cream

Arrange apple slices in a buttered 9"x9" glass baking pan. Drizzle with water; sprinkle with cinnamon and set aside. In a bowl, rub together flour, sugar and butter until crumbly. Spoon flour mixture over apples. Bake at 350 degrees for 40 minutes, or until golden and apples are tender. Serve warm, garnished as desired. Makes 4 to 6 servings.

Create a heavenly glaze for any apple dessert. Melt together
1/2 cup butterscotch chips, 2 tablespoons butter and
2 tablespoons whipping cream over low heat.

Walnut-Topped Carrot Pie

Paula Marchesi
Lenhartsville, PA

I enjoy baking all kinds of sweet goodies for my family. Having a lot of carrots one year from our garden, I decided to try my luck and make a carrot pie. It turned out so well that it's now a staple in our family...this is one tasty pie!

4 c. carrots, peeled and sliced	1/2 t. cinnamon
14-oz. can sweetened condensed milk	1/8 t. salt
	9-inch pie crust, baked
3-oz. pkg. cream cheese, softened	1 c. chopped walnuts
	1/3 c. brown sugar, packed
2 eggs, beaten	3 T. butter, melted
1 t. pumpkin pie spice	

Bring one inch of water to boil in a large saucepan over medium-high heat. Add carrots; reduce heat to medium-low. Cover and cook 10 to 12 minutes, until carrots are tender. Drain and cool. Combine carrots, condensed milk, cream cheese, eggs, spices and salt in a blender. Process until puréed; process one minute longer. Pour carrot mixture into baked pie crust. In a bowl, combine walnuts, brown sugar and melted butter; sprinkle over filling. Bake at 375 degrees for 45 to 50 minutes, until a knife tip inserted near the center tests clean and edges are golden. If necessary, cover edges of crust with aluminum foil during the last 20 minutes of baking to prevent overbrowning. Cool pie on a wire rack before slicing. Makes 6 to 8 servings.

A plain angel food cake is anything but plain when the center's filled with fresh fruit...what could be quicker? Even better, angel food is fat-free and lower in calories than most cakes. Enjoy!

Timeless Treats

Avocado Chiffon Pie

*Katherine Nelson
Centerville, UT*

Even if you don't like avocados, you will love this pie. It's so light and yummy...one of my favorites! I got this recipe 25 years ago from my sister-in-law Judy, while visiting her in Honolulu. She had clipped this recipe from the local newspaper when it was announced as a winner in a pie baking contest. It's still a winner!

1 c. avocado, halved, pitted
    and mashed
3 eggs, separated
1-1/2 T. butter, sliced
1/2 t. nutmeg
1 t. cinnamon

juice of 1/2 lemon
1 c. sugar, divided
1 env. unflavored gelatin
1/4 c. water
9-inch pie crust, baked
Garnish: whipped cream

In a large saucepan, combine avocado, egg yolks, butter, spices, lemon juice and 1/2 cup sugar. Cook over low heat, stirring often, until mixture is hot. Remove from heat. In a cup, dissolve gelatin in water; add to avocado mixture and let cool. In a bowl, beat egg whites with remaining sugar until stiff; fold into avocado mixture. Pour into baked pie crust; cover and chill. Top with whipped cream at serving time. Makes 6 to 8 servings.

Need a special tablecloth for a dessert buffet? There are
so many charming print fabrics in many colors available at the
craft store. Two to three yards is all you'll need. No hemming
required...just trim the edges with pinking shears!

195

Grandma's Pineapple Dream Cake
Emily Farley
Franklin, OH

This is a hit recipe my Grandma Josie Farley made often. She was a strong lady from the mountains of West Virginia and boy, could she cook! She was the head cook at a school for many years. Not only could she cook, she always had a love for her family and would give you the shirt off her back! I hope this recipe brings you joy like it did for our family.

15-1/4 oz. pkg. yellow cake mix
20-oz. can crushed pineapple
1 c. sugar
8-oz. pkg. cream cheese,
    softened
3-3/4 oz. pkg. instant vanilla
    pudding mix

1-1/2 c. milk
3/4 c. shredded coconut, divided
1/2 c. chopped pecans, divided
8-oz. container frozen whipped
    topping, thawed

Prepare cake mix according to package directions, adding ingredients called for. Bake in a greased 13"x9" glass baking pan according to package directions. Meanwhile, in a saucepan over medium heat, combine undrained pineapple and sugar. Bring to a boil, stirring often. Spread hot pineapple mixture over hot cake; let cool. In a bowl, stir together cream cheese, dry pudding mix and milk until smooth and spreadable; spread over cake. Sprinkle half each of coconut and pecans over cake. Frost with whipped topping; sprinkle with remaining coconut and pecans. Cut into squares. Makes 15 servings.

Once in a young lifetime, one should be allowed to have
as much sweetness as one can possibly want and hold.
- Judith Olney

Honey Pineapple Upside-Down Cake

Brenda Trnka
Manitoba, Canada

Mom loved to make this for our Sunday dinner dessert. I was one of seven kids, and we each had to have a cherry!

1/3 c. honey
3 T. margarine
9 slices canned pineapple, drained

9 maraschino cherries
15-1/4 oz. pkg. yellow cake mix

Grease a 9" round cake pan or a 9"x9" baking pan; set aside. Melt honey and margarine in a small saucepan over medium heat; pour into cake pan. Arrange pineapple slices in pan; add a cherry to the center of each slice. Prepare cake mix according to package directions, adding ingredients called for. Slowly spoon batter over fruit. Bake at 350 degrees for 50 to 55 minutes, until cake tests done with a toothpick. Invert pan onto a serving plate. Leave pan in place for 5 minutes; turn cake out onto plate. Makes 8 to 10 servings.

Use fresh pineapple in season to make an upside-down cake even more scrumptious! Cut off the pineapple's top and bottom, stand it upright and slice off the peel all around with a serrated knife. Then slice the pineapple crosswise and trim out the core with a paring knife to form rings.

Spiced Applesauce Cake

Desiree Harris
Roslyn, WA

I tweaked a recipe to create my own fruit-filled version. I love that the cake is so moist and flavorful, yet uses only a little butter. It just proves that you don't need all that fat to make a great cake! I have sent this to work with my husband at the Fire Department several times and it always gets rave reviews. I don't frost this cake because it is yummy as is.

1/2 c. butter, softened
2 eggs, beaten
1-1/2 c. unsweetened natural
  applesauce
2-1/2 c. all-purpose flour
1-1/4 c. brown sugar, packed, or
  white sugar
3/4 t. baking powder
1-1/2 t. baking soda
1 t. salt

1/2 c. water
1 t. vanilla extract
1-1/2 t. apple pie spice
1 t. cinnamon
1/2 t. ground cardamom
1/2 c. raisins
1/2 c. dried cranberries
1 c. canned pears, chopped
1 c. canned peaches, chopped

In a large bowl, combine butter, eggs and applesauce; beat together until smooth. Add remaining ingredients except fruits; stir until combined. Stir in fruits. Pour into a 13"x9" baking pan coated with non-stick vegetable spray. Bake at 350 degrees for 45 to 50 minutes, until a toothpick inserted in the center tests clean. Cut into squares. Makes 12 to 15 servings.

For plump, juicy raisins, cover them with boiling water and let stand for 15 minutes. Drain and pat dry before adding to a recipe.

Amazing Pound Cake

Shirley Morris
Clarks Summit, PA

My father and I worked on this recipe until we got it just right.
Once my father-in-law took a burnt one out of the trash, carved
away the bad part and ate the cake inside...that's how good it is!

1 c. butter
2 c. sugar
2-1/4 c. all-purpose flour
6 eggs

juice of 2 lemons
1 t. vanilla extract
1/8 t. salt

Combine butter and sugar in a large bowl. Beat with an electric mixer on low speed until blended; set aside. To butter mixture, alternately add flour and eggs, one at a time. Add remaining ingredients; beat on medium speed until thick. Pour batter into a greased and floured tube pan. Bake at 300 degrees for one hour and 20 minutes, or until a toothpick inserted near the center tests clean. Cool in pan for for 10 minutes; turn out onto a wire rack and cool completely. Makes 8 to 10 servings.

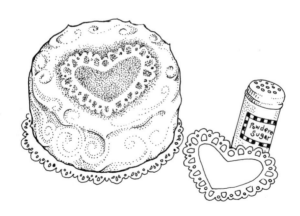

Garnish cakes, cupcakes or cookies in a jiffy...sprinkle
powdered sugar or cocoa through a doily.

Secret-Recipe Birthday Cake

Sara Voges
Washington, IN

This is my super-secret, super-moist, better-than-a-bakery birthday cake. My kids love this fluffy icing too! Sometimes I will whip up some of the icing and just serve it with fruit...it's that good.

16-1/2 oz. pkg. French vanilla
   cake mix
3.4-oz. pkg. French vanilla
   instant pudding mix

2 c. milk
2 eggs, beaten

In a large bowl, stir together dry cake and pudding mixes, milk and eggs. Beat with an electric mixer on high speed for 2 minutes. Spread batter in a greased 13"x9" baking pan. Bake at 350 degrees for 20 minutes, or until a toothpick inserted in center tests done. Cool; top with Whipped Icing. Makes 1 to 18 servings.

Whipped Icing:

3.4-oz pkg. French vanilla
   instant pudding mix
1 c. milk

8-oz. container frozen whipped
   topping, thawed

In a bowl, whisk together dry pudding mix and milk until thickened. Fold in whipped topping. Cover and refrigerate for one to 2 hours before using.

Keep plastic wrap from sticking to a frosted cake. Stick mini marshmallows on the ends of toothpicks, then insert into the cake. Gently cover with plastic wrap...the toothpicks won't poke holes through the wrap!

Timeless Treats

Gran Jan's Ice Cream Brownies

Janice Fry
Hoover, AL

I love to make this for holidays and when the grandkids come over. I had written under the recipe: "This was the hit of Bible School workers in 1996! Everyone loved it!" And, of course, for the next few years I was asked to take it for the helpers at church. It's a great dessert to make ahead during the holidays when you are busy. It's delicious, easy and everybody loves it!

23.6-oz. pkg. fudge
  brownie mix

1/2 gal. vanilla ice cream,
  softened

Prepare brownie mix according to package directions, adding ingredients called for. Bake in a lightly greased 13"x9" baking pan; let cool in pan. Spread ice cream over brownies; cover and freeze until hardened. Spread Chocolate Frosting over ice cream; cover again and return to freezer. Remove from freezer 5 to 10 minutes before serving. Cut into squares. Makes 12 to 15 servings.

Chocolate Frosting:

1-1/2 c. evaporated milk
1/2 c. butter, sliced
2/3 c. semi-sweet chocolate
  chips

2 c. powdered sugar
1 t. vanilla extract
1-1/2 c. chopped pecans
  or walnuts

In a large saucepan over medium-high heat, combine evaporated milk, butter, chocolate chips and powdered sugar. Bring to a boil, stirring until smooth. Reduce heat to medium and cook for 8 minutes. Remove from heat; stir in vanilla and nuts. Let cool before using.

For perfectly cut ice cream treats, line the baking pan with parchment paper before filling it. Once the ice cream has frozen, lift it out onto a cutting board and slice it neatly.

Beth's Chocolate Cake

Barbara Cadwell
The Dalles, OR

*My sister Beth gave me this easy one-bowl recipe. It's the only one
my children would eat! If I tried a different chocolate cake recipe,
they didn't like it and would ask for Auntie Beth's instead.*

1 c. milk
1 t. white vinegar
2-1/2 c. all-purpose flour
1-1/2 c. sugar
1/2 c. baking cocoa
2 t. baking soda
1 t. salt

1/2 c. water
1 t. vanilla extract
2/3 c. butter, melted and slightly
   cooled
2 eggs, beaten
Garnish: favorite frosting

Combine milk and vinegar in a cup; set aside. In a large bowl, combine
flour, sugar, cocoa, baking soda and salt; mix well. Add milk mixture,
water, vanilla and melted butter; mix well. Add eggs. Beat with an
electric mixer on high speed for 2 to 3 minutes. Pour batter into a
greased and floured 13"x9" baking pan. Bake at 350 degrees for
35 minutes, or until a toothpick tests clean. For cupcakes, fill paper-
lined muffin cups 2/3 full; bake for 20 minutes. Cool and frost as
desired. Makes 12 to 15 servings.

Fluffy Cocoa Frosting

Jan Covington
Newport, TN

*This scrumptious recipe is from an old cocoa tin that my mother had.
My brothers Jerry, Charles and I loved it. It's shared in Mom's and
Charles's memory.*

3/4 c. baking cocoa
4 c. powdered sugar
1/2 c. margarine

1 t. vanilla extract
1/2 c. evaporated milk, divided

In a large bowl, mix cocoa and powdered sugar. In a separate bowl,
stir margarine until creamy; add some of cocoa mixture and mix well.
Blend in vanilla and 1/4 cup milk. Add remaining cocoa mixture; stir
well. Add remaining milk; beat to desired consistency. Additional milk
may be added if required, one to 2 drops at a time. Makes enough
frosting for one sheet cake or a 2-layer cake.

Timeless Treats

Cookies & Cream Ice Cream Squares

Pat Beach
Fisherville, KY

This has been our all-time family favorite dessert recipe for over 35 years. It is yummy and super-easy to make.

1/2 gal. vanilla ice cream
8-oz. container frozen whipped
   topping, thawed

18-oz. pkg. chocolate sandwich
   cookies, crushed

Place frozen ice cream in a large bowl; let stand at room temperature until softened. Fold whipped topping into ice cream; fold in crushed cookies. Spoon into a 13"x9" baking pan. Cover and freeze until firm. Cut into squares. Makes 12 to 15 servings.

Orange Ice Cream Pops

Irene Robinson
Cincinnati, OH

Flavorful summertime treats the kids will love.

2 c. vanilla ice cream, softened
1 c. milk
6-oz. can frozen orange juice
   concentrate, thawed

12 frozen treat molds or
   3-oz. disposable plastic cups
12 wooden treat sticks

In a blender, combine ice cream, milk and orange juice. Process until smooth. Pour 1/4 cup into each mold or cup; insert sticks. Freeze until firm. Makes 12 servings.

For party fun, tuck wrapped ice cream sandwiches and other frozen goodies into a pail filled with crushed ice to keep them frosty.

Mom's Date Cake with Chocolate-Nut Topping

Gerri Roth
Flushing, MI

My mom was a home economics teacher and had many wonderful recipes. This was one of my favorites. She showed me how to make this dessert when I was only a child.

1-1/4 c. dates, finely chopped
1 c. hot water
1/4 c. shortening
1 c. plus 2 T. sugar, divided
1 egg, beaten
1 t. vanilla extract

1-2/3 c. all-purpose flour
1 t. baking soda
1/2 t. salt
1 c. chopped pecans, divided
1/2 c. semi-sweet chocolate
    chips

Combine dates and hot water in a bowl; let cool. Meanwhile, in a large bowl, combine shortening, one cup sugar, egg and vanilla. Beat with an electric mixer on high speed for 5 minutes; set aside. In a separate bowl, mix flour, baking soda and salt. Beating on low speed, add flour mixture to shortening mixture alternately with date mixture. Beat just until smooth; fold in 1/2 cup pecans. Pour batter into a greased and floured 9"x9" baking pan. In a small bowl, combine chocolate chips, remaining pecans and remaining sugar; sprinkle over batter. Bake at 350 degrees for 40 to 45 minutes, until a toothpick inserted in center tests clean. Makes 9 servings.

A handy trick for greasing and flouring baking pans... grease the pan, sprinkle with flour, cover with plastic wrap and give it a good shake!

204

Sharon's No-Bake Chocolate Tart

Sharon Jones
Oklahoma City, OK

This is a super-healthy treat that doesn't require you to turn on the stove and it is absolutely delish!

1 c. shredded coconut
3/4 c. raw almonds, ground
1/3 c. baking cocoa

1/3 c. coconut oil
1/4 c. agave nectar

Combine all ingredients in a bowl; mix well. Press mixture into an ungreased 9" tart pan or pie plate to form a crust. Cover and chill for 30 minutes. Pour Filling onto chilled tart shell. Chill another 2 hours, or until firm. To serve, cut into small wedges. Makes 8 to 10 servings.

Filling:

1 c. coconut oil
1 c. baking cocoa

1/4 c. agave nectar
1/2 c. almond butter

In a food processor, blend all ingredients until smooth.

A simple treat...dip banana slices into melted chocolate and then roll in mini chocolate chips. Place on a baking sheet and freeze to make a frosty snack.

Debbie's Pumpkin Pie Custard

Debbie Blundi
Kunkletown, PA

My friends know I love to turn the recipes we grew up with into healthy ones. I had a lot of requests to do something with the old favorite, pumpkin pie. My husband loves it. I have also taken this pie to church meals and nobody could tell the difference between the old and the new! It's sugar, dairy, soy and gluten-free.

3 c. dates, coarsely chopped
1 to 2 c. coconut milk
4 c. canned pumpkin
2 t. allspice or pumpkin pie spice
1 T. baking soda

1 T. gluten-free flour
1 t. vanilla extract
Optional: 2 9-inch gluten-free
    pie crusts, baked

Place dates in a food processor. Process with enough coconut milk to make a paste. Transfer date paste to a large bowl. Add remaining ingredients except crusts. Beat with an electric mixer on medium speed for 2 minutes. Pour mixture into 2 baked pie crusts, or 9" baking pans without crusts. Bake at 350 degrees for one hour, or until tops turn golden and start to crack and a knife tip inserted into centers tests clean. Makes 2 pies or custards, 8 servings each.

Make a luscious non-dairy whipped topping from full-fat coconut cream. Chill an unopened can overnight. Open it and scoop the thickened cream into a bowl, discarding liquid. Beat with an electric mixer on high speed for 30 seconds. Add honey and vanilla extract to taste; beat for one minute. Use immediately, or cover and refrigerate up to one week.

Timeless Treats

Old-Fashioned Angel Pie

Nancy Wolff
Bridgewater Corners, VT

This recipe for a meringue dessert originally came from my husband's grandmother. She was an excellent cook and we enjoyed many meals around her table. I can still remember how impressed our guests were the first time I made this recipe as a newlywed!

1/4 t. salt	1/2 t. vanilla extract
1/4 t. cream of tartar	Garnish: whipped cream
4 egg whites	Optional: fresh berries
1 c. sugar	

In a deep bowl, add salt and cream of tartar to egg whites. Beat with an electric mixer on high speed until stiff peaks form. Beat in sugar, one tablespoon at a time; beat in vanilla. Spread in a well buttered 9" pie plate, spreading mixture higher around the edge to make a rim. Bake at 275 degrees for one hour, or until meringue is lightly golden, dry and firm to the touch. Let cool. Spread meringue with whipped cream. If desired, garnish with berries. Makes 8 servings.

Deliver a tray of cookies and fresh fruit to a nursing home, an elderly neighbor or a friend who needs cheering.

207

Banana Drop Cookies

Stephanie Mullen
Rock Springs, WY

My mom got this recipe from her mom. These are the softest cookies I have ever had. After you've tried them, you won't go back to ordinary chocolate chip cookies! I always have to double the recipe... they vanish quickly. They're a wonderful treat to bake for family & friends.

2/3 c. butter-flavored shortening	1/4 t. baking soda
1 c. sugar	1/2 t. salt
2 eggs	3 very ripe bananas, mashed
2-1/2 c. all-purpose flour	1/2 t. vanilla extract
2 t. baking powder	1 c. semi-sweet chocolate chips

Beat shortening in a large bowl; gradually beat in sugar. Beat in eggs, one at a time; set aside. In a separate bowl, mix flour, baking powder, baking soda and salt. To shortening mixture, alternately add flour mixture and bananas until well mixed. Stir in vanilla and chocolate chips. Drop batter by teaspoonfuls onto greased baking sheets. Bake at 350 degrees for about 12 minutes. Makes 3 dozen.

A heaping plate of cupcakes, cookies or bars makes a delightful and delicious centerpiece at a casual gathering with friends... don't forget the napkins!

208

Honey & Whole-Wheat Cookies   *JoAnn*

We love these crisp cookies with a hint of citrus!

2 c. whole-wheat flour
1 T. powdered milk
1 t. baking powder
1/2 t. baking soda
1/2 t. nutmeg
1/2 c. butter, sliced

1/2 c. honey
1 T. lemon or orange zest
1 T. vanilla extract
1 egg, beaten
1/2 t. cinnamon

In a large bowl, combine flour, powdered milk, baking powder, baking soda and nutmeg. Cut in butter with 2 table knives; set aside. In a separate bowl, beat together honey, zest, vanilla and egg; add to flour mixture. Mix well and form dough into one-inch balls. Place balls on a baking sheet, 2 inches apart; flatten each slightly with a fork. Sprinkle with cinnamon. Bake at 375 degrees for 8 to 10 minutes, until lightly golden with soft centers. Makes 2 to 3 dozen.

An old secret for keeping cookies moist...slip a slice of bread
into the cookie jar!

Chocolatey Cottage Cheese Cookies

Brenda Kauffman
Harrisburg, PA

My mother-in-law gave me this recipe when we were first married. It's a delicious chewy, chocolatey cookie.

2/3 c. butter, softened
1-2/3 c. sugar
1 c. cottage cheese
2 eggs, beaten
2 t. vanilla extract
2-3/4 c. all-purpose flour

1/2 c. baking cocoa
1 t. baking powder
1/2 t. baking soda
1/2 t. salt
Garnish: powdered sugar

In a large bowl, combine all ingredients except powdered sugar; mix well. Cover and chill dough for 2 to 3 hours. Form dough into balls by tablespoonfuls; roll in powdered sugar. Place on greased baking sheets. Bake at 350 degrees for 7 to 9 minutes, until golden. Makes about 3-1/2 dozen.

Fudgy Mocha Brownies

Kathy Kyler
Norman, OK

This was originally a recipe from a friend...I added my own tweaks for a mocha twist! These brownies keep well, and are very rich. They are also good if you omit the espresso powder and substitute mint chips for chocolate chips.

1-1/2 c. all-purpose flour
2 c. sugar
1/2 t. baking powder
1/2 c. baking cocoa
1/2 to 1 t. espresso powder
1/4 t. salt

1 c. butter, melted and cooled
  slightly
4 eggs, beaten
1 t. vanilla extract
2 c. semi-sweet chocolate chips

In a large bowl, whisk together flour, sugar, baking powder, baking cocoa, espresso powder and salt. In a separate bowl, stir together melted butter, eggs and vanilla; add to flour mixture. Stir well. Fold in chocolate chips. Pour batter into a buttered 13"x9" baking pan. Bake at 350 degrees for 30 to 35 minutes. Let cool and cut into squares. Makes 2 dozen.

Gluten-Free Drop Sugar Cookies

Amanda Carlisle
Palm Coast, FL

My son Mason was diagnosed with a wheat allergy and my daughter Audrey with a dairy allergy. It has made baking a challenge for me. In order to keep things normal for them, I came up with this sugar cookie recipe. These cookies are so good, you honestly can't tell they're gluten-free!

1/2 c. butter-flavored shortening
   or margarine
1 c. sugar
1 egg
1 t. vanilla extract

1-1/3 c. gluten-free biscuit
   baking mix
3/4 t. baking powder
1/4 t. salt

Combine shortening or margarine and sugar in a large bowl. Beat with an electric mixer on medium speed until light and fluffy. Beat in egg and vanilla until blended. Reduce mixer speed to low and add remaining ingredients; beat until well mixed. Drop dough by heaping teaspoonfuls onto a parchment paper-lined baking sheet, 2 inches apart. Bake at 350 degrees for 10 minutes, or just until golden around the edges. Cool. Makes about 1-1/2 to 2 dozen.

Cookies can be wrapped individually to place in goody bags or give as classroom treats. You can even turn them into cookie pops...frost in pairs with a wooden treat stick placed in between.

No-Bake Raspberry Lemon Bars

Shirl Parsons
Cape Carteret, NC

My dear friend Ms. Nola gave me this great 1950s recipe that had been handed down from her mother. Her mom made these yummy cookie bars often when she was a child.

12 graham cracker squares, crushed
2 T. butter, melted
2 8-oz. pkgs. fat-free cream cheese

7-oz. jar marshmallow creme
1 T. lemon juice
2 c. fresh raspberries, divided

In a bowl, toss together cracker crumbs and melted butter. Press into an ungreased 9"x9" baking pan. Cover and refrigerate crust while making filling. Combine cream cheese, marshmallow creme and lemon juice in a separate large bowl. Beat with an electric mixer on medium speed until light and fluffy. Reserve 16 raspberries for garnish. Gently stir in remaining raspberries; spoon onto crust. Cover and refrigerate 4 hours. Cut into 16 bars; top each bar with a raspberry. Makes 16 bars.

Arrange home-baked goodies on a tiered cake stand
for a delightful dessert tray that doesn't take up
much space on a buffet.

Lemon Shortbread Triangles

Lisa Johnson
Hallsville, TX

This shortbread cookie recipe has been in the family for some time. My mama has had it for several years and has made some adjustments to the ingredients. These cookies are scrumptious!

1-1/4 c. butter, softened
3/4 c. powdered sugar
2-3/4 c. all-purpose flour
1 t. ginger
1/2 c. mixed nuts, finely
   chopped

1 c. mixed nuts, coarsely
   chopped
1/2 c. white chocolate chips

In a large bowl, stir together butter and powdered sugar until fluffy. Add flour, ginger and finely chopped nuts; mix well. Press dough into an ungreased rimmed baking sheet with a one-inch rim. Sprinkle with coarsely chopped nuts and chocolate chips; press lightly into dough. Bake at 325 degrees for 25 minutes, or until edges are golden. Remove from oven. Cut into squares; cut squares diagonally, to form triangles. Drizzle Lemon Glaze over entire pan of shortbread. Cool completely in the pan. Makes about 2 dozen.

Lemon Glaze:

1 c. powdered sugar
1 t. lemon zest

4 t. lemon juice

In a bowl, mix together all ingredients until smooth.

Sweet take-home favors for a ladies' luncheon! Fill delicate flowered vintage teacups with scented wax crystals and slip in a wick.

Oatmeal-Lime Cookies with Chocolate Chunks

Jonni Sue Wilhelm
Hebron, MD

This is a sugar-free recipe I created to serve at our church's coffee shop. There are many requests for sugar-free goodies and this cookie is a hit! You can make it with sugar, but it is delicious the way it is.

1/2 c. butter, softened
1-1/4 c. low-calorie brown sugar
    blend for baking, or 2/3 c.
    light brown sugar, packed
1 egg, beaten
1/2 t. vanilla extract
1 T. lime zest
1-1/2 T. lime juice
3/4 c. all-purpose flour

1/2 t. baking soda
1/2 t. kosher salt
1/2 t. cinnamon
1/2 t. nutmeg
1-1/2 c. rolled oats, uncooked
1 c. sugar-free chocolate bars,
    chopped
Optional: 1/2 c. chopped
    walnuts, 3/4 c. raisins

In a large bowl, blend together butter, brown sugar, egg and vanilla until smooth. Add lime zest and lime juice; mix well. In a separate bowl, whisk together flour, baking soda, salt and spices. Stir flour mixture into butter mixture; blend well. Stir in oats, chocolate, walnuts and raisins, if using. Scoop dough by rounded tablespoonfuls onto parchment paper-lined baking sheets, 2 inches apart. Place baking sheets in the freezer for 15 minutes to chill dough. Bake at 325 degrees for 10 to 12 minutes, until edges are golden and tops look slightly undercooked. Let cookies stand on hot baking sheets for 5 minutes more to finish baking. Makes 2 to 2-1/2 dozen.

Dress up homemade cookies
in a snap! Simply use a fork
to drizzle cookies with
melted white chocolate.

Timeless Treats

No-Bake Orange Balls

Samantha Reilly
Gig Harbor, WA

This recipe has been enjoyed by four generations of my family. It is a bit of a mess to make, but kids love to make it and they taste so good that the clean-up is worth it. We used to make them every year for my grandpa & grandma as well as my great-grandpa & great-grandma. Now that they have passed on, this recipe always makes me think of them. Happy memories!

12-oz. pkg. vanilla wafers, crushed
16-oz. pkg. powdered sugar, sifted
1/2 c. butter, melted

6-oz. can frozen orange juice concentrate, thawed
14-oz. can sweetened condensed milk
7-oz. pkg. shredded coconut

Place a wire rack over a length of wax paper; set aside. In a large bowl, combine vanilla wafer crumbs and powdered sugar. Stir in melted butter and orange juice; set aside. Pour condensed milk into a shallow dish. Pour coconut into another shallow dish. Form crumb mixture into walnut-size balls. Dip balls into condensed milk, coating on all sides; dip into coconut, coating on all sides. Place balls on a wire rack to dry. When dry, store in an airtight container up to 1-1/2 weeks; keep covered. Makes 4 to 5 dozen.

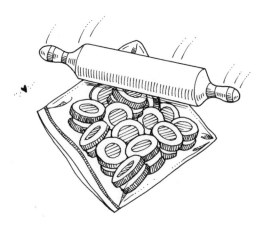

Crush vanilla wafers or graham crackers quickly...place them in a plastic zipping bag and roll over them with a rolling pin.

Gluten-Free Date Balls

Marian Forck
Chamois, MO

*My daughter Sarah has always loved date balls, but she is
following a gluten-free diet now. So, I came up with
these yummy treats for her.*

2 eggs, beaten
2/3 c. sugar
2 T. butter
1 c. chopped dates
1/8 t. salt

1 t. vanilla extract
1 c. chopped nuts
2 c. bite-size crispy rice cereal
   squares, crushed
7-oz. pkg. shredded coconut

In a large saucepan over low heat, combine eggs, sugar, butter, dates
and salt. Cook and stir for 7 minutes. Remove from heat; stir in
vanilla, nuts and cereal. Form into one-inch balls. Place coconut in a
shallow dish; coat balls in coconut. Store in an airtight container.
Makes 3 dozen.

Use kitchen shears to make short work of cutting up dates,
apricots and other sticky cookie ingredients.

Timeless Treats

Peanut Butter Cookies on the Light Side

Beckie Apple
Grannis, AR

I have lived with diabetes for many years and I am always looking for ways to re-invent recipes so I can enjoy them. These cookies taste really good and the whole family likes them.

1 c. creamy or crunchy peanut
   butter
3 T. brown sugar, packed
3 T. sugar-free pancake syrup
1 egg, beaten

1/2 t. vanilla extract
3 T. self-rising flour
1/2 c. no-calorie powdered
   sweetener for baking

In a bowl, combine peanut butter, brown sugar, syrup, egg and vanilla; blend well. Add flour and sweetener; mix well. Form dough into one-inch balls. Place on a baking sheet coated with non-stick vegetable spray. Flatten with fork tines to form 2-inch cookies. Bake at 350 degrees for 6 to 8 minutes. Let cool completely before removing from baking sheet. Makes 2 dozen.

Amazing Peanut Butter Cookies

Nancy Lanning
Lancaster, SC

Since our daughter Rebekah needs to be gluten-free, we make these cookies often....we all love them. They really are amazing!

1 c. creamy peanut butter
1/2 c. brown sugar, packed
1/2 c. sugar
1 egg, beaten

1 t. baking soda
Optional: 1/2 c. semi-sweet
   chocolate chips
Garnish: sugar

In a bowl, mix all ingredients except garnish. Form dough into balls by tablespoonfuls; roll balls in sugar. Place on a parchment paper-lined baking sheet; do not press down. Bake at 350 degrees for 10 to 12 minutes. Let cool on baking sheet; remove to a wire rack. Makes 15.

INDEX

INDEX

Desserts

Mains

INDEX

Find Gooseberry Patch
wherever you are!

www.gooseberrypatch.com

Email

Blog

You Tube

Call us toll-free at 1·800·854·6673

U.S. to Metric Recipe Equivalents

Volume Measurements

1/4 teaspoon	1 mL
1/2 teaspoon	2 mL
1 teaspoon	5 mL
1 tablespoon = 3 teaspoons	15 mL
2 tablespoons = 1 fluid ounce	30 mL
1/4 cup	60 mL
1/3 cup	75 mL
1/2 cup = 4 fluid ounces	125 mL
1 cup = 8 fluid ounces	250 mL
2 cups = 1 pint =16 fluid ounces	500 mL
4 cups = 1 quart	1 L

Weights

1 ounce	30 g
4 ounces	120 g
8 ounces	225 g
16 ounces = 1 pound	450 g

Oven Temperatures

300° F	150° C
325° F	160° C
350° F	180° C
375° F	190° C
400° F	200° C
450° F	230° C

Baking Pan Sizes

Square	
8x8x2 inches	2 L = 20x20x5 cm
9x9x2 inches	2.5 L = 23x23x5 cm
Rectangular	
13x9x2 inches	3.5 L = 33x23x5 cm

Loaf	
9x5x3 inches	2 L = 23x13x7 cm
Round	
8x1-1/2 inches	1.2 L = 20x4 cm
9x1-1/2 inches	1.5 L = 23x4 cm